Know Your Rights
Consumer Rights

'In the minefield that is modern living, the consumer is supposed to be king – the truth of course is very different. The reality is that consumers are the softest of targets, the easiest of marks.... Well armed with Andrew McCann's *Know Your Rights: Consumer Rights*, you will never again be fobbed off, short-changed or patronised by a shop assistant or jobsworth'

Mark Cagney, Presenter of Ireland AM, *TV3*

'Whether dealing with your landlord, local government or supermarket, here it is: your bill of rights'

Kevin Myers, Journalist

'In these times, more than ever, it is vital that the citizen is empowered by knowledge of their rights and entitlements. Andrew McCann's *Know Your Rights: Consumer Rights* is an indispensable guide'

Ivan Yates, Broadcaster

'This timely and accessible guide to public and private services is commendable'

Emily O'Reilly, Ombudsman and Information Commissioner

'We've consulted Andrew McCann many times on our programme and have found him to be a human encyclopaedia of relevant information about the issues which concern Irish people. *Know Your Rights: Consumer Rights* is an extension of Andrew's vast knowledge and I thoroughly recommend it to all Irish citizens, particularly those trying to wade their way through the myriad of 'red tape' obstacles which our modern society has created.'

David Harvey, Presenter, Classic Hits 4FM

'This is the book you need on your shelf at a time when every purchase matters, every bill hurts, every cent counts and every class of a chancer is trying to part you from your cash. Andrew is the go-to guy for straight-talking consumer advice – this book is one investment you won't regret'

Brenda Power, Journalist, Sunday Times

'When it comes to social and civic rights in Ireland, Andrew McCann is the king. *Know Your Rights: Consumer Rights* will empower readers to make the correct decisions for their circumstances'

Margaret E. Ward, Broadcaster and Journalist

Know Your Rights
Consumer Rights

Andrew McCann

ORPEN PRESS

Orpen Press
Lonsdale House
Avoca Avenue
Blackrock
Co. Dublin
Ireland

e-mail: info@orpenpress.com
www.orpenpress.com

Paperback ISBN: 978-1-871305-28-9
ePub ISBN: 978-1-871305-63-0
Kindle ISBN: 978-1-871305-64-7

Printed in the UK by the MPG Books Group

This book is dedicated to my Mam, Phyllis (Catherine) McCann, who always advised me to complete my studies before I got involved with women. Thankfully I did!

Disclaimer and Waiver of Liability

Contents

Introduction xi

Chapter 1   Consumer Rights – Goods and Services.....   1
  Goods..   1
  Defective Items...   3
  Non-Defective Items..   11
  Purchasing Items in a Sale..   14
  Credit Notes...   15
  Guarantees..   16
  Misleading Advice from Shop Staff............................   19
  Food Labelling..   20
  Pricing..   21
  Deliveries   24
  Purchasing Goods Privately.......................................   25
  Services...   27
  Holidays and Travel...   33
          Passports...   33
          Air Travel   34
          Travelling to and from the US..........................   41
          Package Holidays...   41
          Driving Abroad/Car Rental.............................   44
          Sickness and Death Abroad   47
  Consumer Rights – General   50
          EU Consumer Rights Directive and Pending
          Consumer Rights Act 2012................................   50

Contents

Shopping Online... 52
Data Protection.. 55
Misleading Claims and Advertising 59
Signs and Notices 62
Gift Vouchers... 63
Legal Tender 65
Deposits 66
Purchasing by Credit... 67

Chapter 2   Consumer Complaints **71**
Formal Complaints... 71
Sample Letter (Goods) 72
Sample Letter (Services)..................................... 74
Small Claims Court 76
Where to Complain 80
Broadcasting (TV/Radio)................................... 80
Builders... 81
Car Insurance 82
Cold Calling... 84
Dentists... 84
Doctors.. 85
Driving Instructors 87
Electricity Providers.. 87
Financial Services... 89
Food Safety.. 90
Gardaí 91
Health Insurance 93
Licensed Premises... 96
Motor Industry... 98
Nursing Homes 100
Pensions.. 101
Pharmacists.. 102
Private Health Insurance.................................... 103
Press... 104
Solicitors 104
Taxi Regulator.. 106
Telecom Providers... 107

Contents

Chapter 3   Property Rights.................................... **111**
Affordable Housing.. 111
Renting 118
    Rental Accommodation Scheme 119
    Landlord and Tenant Rights 121
Management Companies...................................... 130
Energy Rating and Insulation 136
Heating Costs 137
The Household Charge... 139
Second Home Charge (Non-Principal Private
    Residence (NPPR)) 143
Water Charges.. 145
Neighbourhood Nuisance 145
Trespassers.. 153
Occupier's Liability 155
Flooding, Snow, Frost and Ice............................ 157
Equity Release 162
    Lifetime Mortgage Scheme 162
    Home Reversion Schemes 163

Chapter 4   General Citizens' Rights.................... **169**
Begging.. 169
Change of Name 170
Credit History... 171
Data Protection... 172
Debt Collection.. 173
Driving in Ireland 174
First Aid... 179
Freedom of Information....................................... 180
Ombudsman... 182
Irish Citizenship... 183
Money Advice.. 185
TV Licence.. 188
Pets... 189
Voting Rights... 190
Ward of Court 193

Introduction

The idea for *Know Your Rights: Consumer Rights* came from a broad spectrum of directions.

In the last two years I have seen a large increase in the number of consumer-related complaints issues I have had to deal with on TV and radio and in person, and more and more consumers are getting frustrated with the red tape and barriers they are being subjected to.

Also, in light of the current economic climate, consumers are more apprehensive in relation to their purchasing decisions and are taking more time to research those decisions in order to find retailers and suppliers with the best value for money and excellent customer service.

It is estimated that Irish consumers will spend €81 billion in 2012 (Amárach Consulting, 2012); therefore shouldn't consumers fully know their rights and entitlements before and after making these crucial decisions?

This book takes on board some of the topics discussed in the *Know Your Rights* 2010 edition, incorporating all the legislative updates since then, and looks at a wide range of consumer topics in some detail. In Chapter 1 we examine those simple day-to-day consumer rights regarding goods and services issues, including the difference between faulty goods under law and simply a change of mind. We explore the differences in terminology and protection between guarantees and your statutory entitlements. Misleading labelling and pricing are a continuing frustration in our lives and Chapter 1 examines our rights and the complaints process in these areas. We also examine the area of gift vouchers, especially now in light of the increased number of shop and business closures. The proposed changes announced to reform consumer rights across the EU and Ireland are also discussed. Chapter 1 also examines the vast area of travel and holiday rights and protection under EU law.

Chapter 2 discusses how to make a formal complaint and includes sample complaint letters. It also examines the small claims process and the costs involved. The chapter concludes with a list of bodies to which you can complain across a broad range of areas, from complaints in relation to solicitors to those concerning cold calling.

Chapter 3 examines consumer rights in terms of property. Topics discussed include social and affordable housing, housing adaptation grants and supports, the Rental Accommodation Scheme (RAS), neighbourhood nuisances, and, of course, landlord and tenant issues. This chapter also explores the ever-complex area of management companies and the changes in legislation introduced in 2011. We also examine the Household Charge, the second home property charge and the pending water charges.

In Chapter 4 we explore issues of concern to the citizen, including our rights in relation to debt collection, begging and data protection, as well as our entitlement to access information about ourselves and complain about public bodies to the Ombudsman. We also examine issues relating to driving in Ireland, including the NCT, penalty points and car rental.

Know Your Rights: Consumer Rights answers a vast range of topical day-to-day questions relevant to the consumer and citizen. If you have a question that has not been covered in this book, please send it in and I will do my best to address it. Questions should be forwarded to:

Orpen Press
Lonsdale House
Avoca Avenue
Blackrock
Co. Dublin

Tel: 01 2785090
Email: info@orpenpress.com

I can also be contacted through my website: www. yourrights.ie.

CHAPTER 1

Consumer Rights – Goods and Services

Who is a 'consumer' in the eyes of the law?
A consumer is someone who makes a contract (or purchase) with a business and the goods or services purchased are part of that contract, and must be for private use or consumption only (section 3 of the Sale of Goods and Supply of Services Act 1980). This excludes contracts by competitive tender or sale by auction. If there is doubt as to the status of the contract, it must be proven that the relevant party is not acting as a consumer.

Goods

What are 'consumer goods'?
Regulation 2 (Sale of Goods and Associated Guarantees Regulation 2003) defines consumer goods as 'any tangible moveable item'.

I have heard about the National Consumer Agency. What is its role?

The function of the National Consumer Agency (NCA) is to promote and protect the interests and welfare of consumers, enforce consumer law and investigate suspected offences or breaches of law, and to promote possible alternative dispute resolution (ADR) procedures. Authorised officers of the NCA have the power to enter premises, access documentation and other evidence, and apply to the courts for search warrants if required.

Under the Consumer Protection Act 2007, increased powers have been granted to the NCA, which include prosecution, compliance notices, undertakings, prohibition orders and fixed payment notices. The Act also allows (section 31) for the shared use of information between the Competition Authority, the Garda Síochána, the Director of Corporate Enforcement, the Office of Revenue Commissioners, the Central Bank and the Financial Services Authority of Ireland, and any person prescribed by the Minister for Jobs, Enterprise and Innovation.

In addition, the Act imposes price display regulations (section 57), which require traders to display the price or charge to consumers (inclusive of charges, fees or taxes payable – section 57(2)(a)). This requirement applies to food for sale by weight (section 59(2)) and the price must be on prominent display.

It is proposed the National Consumer Agency and the Competition Authority will be amalgamated in 2012 under the Consumer and Competition Bill. The new Bill will also make provision for a statutory code of conduct in the grocery goods sector.

Defective Items

I bought an item in a shop and it does not work. What can I do?

It is advisable not to tamper with the item (tampering may remove any rights), to return it as soon as possible to restrict any acceptance of liability and to ensure you keep the proof of purchase, e.g. the receipt. Goods and services sold by a retailer or provider to a consumer are protected under the Sale of Goods and Supply of Services Act 1980. The Act states:

- Goods must be of merchantable quality, i.e. have a certain standard, and should last a reasonable period in relation to cost (up to six years).
- Goods must be fit for the purpose required, i.e. the purpose and use of the product as described by the manufacturer. If you have specifically asked the seller what the purpose or use of an item is, and they have told you, you have acted in good faith on their specialised opinion (section 10(14)). Under Regulation 5 of the Sale of Consumer Goods and Associated Guarantees Regulation 2003, the seller is bound by public statements regarding the product, i.e. if the product says 'Will help you lose weight', the product must comply with the statement.
- Regulation 6 takes into account problems with installation instructions, thereby causing the goods to be fitted incorrectly. This is classed then as not conforming to requirements.
- Goods must be as described, i.e. the description must comply with the label and its specific purpose. For example, if it is advertised as a waterproof blanket, it must be waterproof (section 10(13)).

- Goods should correspond with a sample, i.e. the delivered item must comply with the sample as displayed (section 10(15)).

If a product does not comply with the above criteria, a customer can claim compensation in the form of one of the 'three Rs':

- Repair
- Replace
- Refund

If the item is new and the fault occurred upon commencement of use or within a very short period, this would appear to be a manufacturing fault. Therefore, in this case, the item should be replaced, repaired as new or the price should be refunded. The decision lies with the seller of the goods. In some cases you could seek to have the item repaired elsewhere, and therefore sue the seller for costs.

The consumer can use whichever of the Acts provides them with the greatest protection: the Sale of Goods and Supply of Services Act 1980 (incorporating the 1893 Act) or the Sale of Consumer Goods and Associated Guarantees Regulation 2003.

I recently purchased an expensive PC. I didn't know which one was the best for me or my requirements. I relied on the salesperson to provide me with the one that met my needs the most. It appears the PC won't do what I want it to do. What redress do I have, if any?

Under section 10(14)(4) of the Sale of Goods and Supply of Services Act, if the buyer of the goods makes known to the salesperson the reason or purpose and use for which the item is being bought, there is a reasonable belief that the goods provided are fit for the purpose intended. Therefore, if the item does not do what it is meant to do, you may seek to return the item to the shop. If you ask for specific assistance or guidance as to your certain needs and a salesperson advises you which products are suitable or not suitable and you purchase a product that is not suitable, this could go against you if you wish to return the product.

When buying goods or services, it is important to fully explain the intended purpose of the item or service sought, as well as to ensure you get the seller's name (and/or details) in case any future problem arises. It may also be advisable to clarify fully the shop's or seller's position if the goods/services do not meet your requirements or suit the purpose.

I bought an iPod recently. Everything went well and I downloaded my music. Two months later a problem occurred, and the screen freezes intermittently. The shop won't take it back now due to some copyright rules. Do I have a case?

Yes, as the item is now faulty, it should be repaired, replaced or refunded. If the item becomes faulty within the first six months it would be classified as a manufacturing fault and the item should be replaced (section 8, S.I. 11/2003, European Communities (Certain Aspects of the Sale of Consumer Goods and Associated Guarantees) Regulations 2003). Alternatively, the item should be repaired or replaced by the seller and/or the manufacturer (under the terms of their guarantee). If the shop is unwilling to do so, they are in breach of your statutory rights and/or the manufacturer's guarantee. The manufacturer's guarantee is an added 'bonus' in addition to your statutory rights (rights under law).

When I brought a faulty item back to the shop, the retailer told me it was the manufacturer's fault. Is this true?
No, this is not true. The seller of the goods is responsible for the goods sold (Sale of Good and Supply of Services Act 1980, section 17). The seller cannot redirect blame for products to the manufacturer and cannot refuse to assist you. The seller, acting as agent to the manufacturer, is responsible for implementing the terms of the guarantee (from the manufacturer). The seller, having sold the item, takes full responsibility for the product. You can take action either against the seller, and/or against the manufacturer for non-implementation of the guarantee. If the manufacturer does not comply with their guarantee, the courts may order observance of the guarantee or award damages (section 19). If you are unsuccessful in gaining co-operation from the seller and s/he refers you to a third party (manufacturer), to whom you may have to pay a call-out charge to investigate a fault, ensure you get a receipt for such payment. You may then take the matter further on grounds of breach of the Sale of Goods and Supply of Services Act 1980 (merchantable quality) and/or breach of guarantee (provided by the manufacturer) (section 19) and request a refund of such costs.

The seller told me that a faulty item should be sent for repair and he won't offer a replacement or refund. What can I do?
As mentioned, faults that occur within the first six months may be classified as manufacturing faults, and a replacement should be given without quibble. Items sent for repair

should generally be items that have worked reliably for a reasonable and satisfactory period and should be returned in the same condition as before the fault occurred.

Under section 12(1), the Sale of Goods and Supply of Services Act 1980 implies a warranty, either from the seller or on behalf of the manufacturer, that spare parts and adequate after-sale service will be made available for a defined period or a reasonable period of time. This period is currently defined, at most, as the period covered under the Statute of Limitations Act 1957 (section 13(8)(ii)), i.e. six years. The period for motor vehicles (section 13) is two years only. In such cases repairs should only be minor and the repair should be completed within a reasonable period of time. If you do accept that the item will be sent off for repair and the item is returned with the same or a similar fault, this gives you, the consumer, a stronger case for a refund or replacement.

Do I need a receipt for a faulty item when I return it to the shop?
Although it is advisable to get one, a receipt is not necessarily required. Proof of purchase is specifically required. Such proof of purchase may include cheque stub, laser receipt or evidence of a credit card transaction as an alternative to a receipt.

Do I need the original packaging? Will I be refused if I do not have it?
No, not necessarily, but it is recommended to have the original packaging if possible. As a consumer, you may have used the product for a period of time and therefore you may have disposed of the original packaging. Returning the item without original packaging does not

remove your statutory rights. Where possible, keep any instruction manuals, manufacturing codes, etc. that may identify a production batch. This may assist with your complaint.

What if an item was marked 'seconds' and a fault occurs? What can I do?

If the item is marked 'seconds' it would be advisable for the seller to specifically highlight the reason the item is 'seconds' (section 14(2)(a) of the Sale of Goods and Supply of Services Act 1980). By highlighting the fact, the seller has brought the issue to your attention. As a consumer, if you accept the reason why the item is 'seconds', this may restrict your possible remedy on the grounds that you were fully aware of and accepted such a situation when purchasing. It is also important, as a consumer, to fully examine any item before buying it as if you notice any defects after purchase that ought to have been found by reasonable examination, you may not be entitled to redress/return (section 10 (14)(2)(b)). However, if a fault occurs that is not related to the item being 'seconds', you are still covered under legislation.

I bought a mobile phone recently and when I returned the item to the shop because it was faulty, the assistant informed me that I have to talk to the manager or send the item to be repaired or assessed. Can he do this?

The assistant should fully assist you, the consumer, with your complaint. All shops or retailers should ideally have a procedure for complaints.

As I stated earlier, if the phone is faulty or has not conformed to the Sale of Goods and Supply of Services Act 1980, and the fault occurred within a short period of time after purchase, it may generally be described as a manufacturer's fault and should be replaced or repaired. It may be that the fault occurred from incorrect use or breakage, and therefore the shop or retailer may have a right to refuse to help you.

In normal cases, the three Rs should apply (in such order: Repair, Replace, Refund). Each case is assessed on its own merits, assuming a suitable agreement has been made between the parties. If the item is to be repaired, it is assumed the repair is minor and it should take a fair and reasonable period of time.

Should the shop provide me with a replacement phone if it is being repaired?

Such a provision is at the discretion of the retailer and the retailer may have policies in place to provide a replacement as a goodwill gesture or for a small fee. Additional warranties may be available for a fee in relation to additional phone cover, e.g. in the event of theft, or possibly under the terms of the seller's and/or manufacturer's guarantee.

I bought an item in a large shop and a fault appeared. When I returned the item and sought a refund, the shop said they would send out a refund cheque. Is this legal?

Ideally, a shop should refund the price of the item in the format paid. Preferably, refunds should be repaid at the time the item is returned.

The Sale of Goods and Supply of Services Act 1980 does not specify that a refund should be paid 'on the spot' or be necessarily through the method by which you originally paid. Therefore, technically, the shop is not compromising your statutory rights. However, you should (if not otherwise informed by the shop before or at the time of purchase) request a refund in the format paid at the time of the return of the item. It would be advisable for retailers to inform customers of their policy and procedure on refunds (exchanges and faulty goods) prior to transactions. Best practice recommends refunds should be facilitated via the original payment method by the customer.

In summary, you do not have an automatic right to a refund at the time of return (subject to the item being faulty), but as a consumer it is always advisable to fully clarify the policy of the shop regarding refunds and, if unhappy, to 'shop around'.

When I brought an item back to the shop, the seller refused to do anything. What can I do?

If, having discussed the item with the seller and having put forward your complaint in a calm and assertive manner, they refuse to assist you, it would then be advisable to put your complaint in writing.

I purchased an electrical item and it caught fire, damaging property in my house. Do I have any comeback?

Yes, it may be possible. Under the Liability for Defective Products Act 1991, the consumer may seek compensation for injury to property (other than the defective product) and physical injury. The consumer needs to show a connection between the damage caused and the product itself (this may be possible via an investigative report). In this situation the manufacturer or producer of the goods is liable, but if the producer or manufacturer cannot be identified, the seller of the goods is liable.

For the item to be classified as 'defective', it must fail to provide the safety expected, taking into consideration failure to warn of possible damage, the purpose the product was used for and the time the product was in circulation. In such cases, for damages to be paid, the cost of the damage must exceed €445. Claims must be made within three years of the damage occurring, or when the person 'reasonably' became aware of it. All actions expire after ten years from the date the product came into circulation.

If I buy a brand new car, is it covered under the Sale of Goods and Supply of Services Act 1980?

Yes, the same principles apply: whether an item is of merchantable quality, is fit for the purpose required, is as described, or whether it is as per sample. The only difference is that the time period for complaints is only two years (compared to six for other goods). It may be advisable to purchase a vehicle from a garage registered with the Society of the Irish Motor Industry (SIMI). The method of redress is the same, i.e. make your complaint in writing to the garage, and if you are still unhappy it may be advisable to make a complaint to the SIMI (if the garage is registered with them). If the matter cannot be resolved, it would be advisable to seek legal opinion, as redress cannot be taken to the Small Claims Court, since the cost of the car is above the upper value limit of €2,000. Any legal action may have to be taken, depending on the value of the vehicle, to the District or Circuit Court.

Non-Defective Items

I bought a dress last week. I washed it and the colour ran. What can I do?

It is important in this case to ensure you fully complied with the washing instructions on the label of the dress. All items must carry a label stating what it is made of and washing and ironing instructions.

If you have not conformed to the requirements, you may not be entitled to a refund or exchange as you, the consumer, may be responsible for such damage. If you have conformed to the instructions, and the item has been affected (this also applies to shrinkage), you are within your rights to seek a remedy for damage caused.

If no washing or care instructions are on an item and you followed steps that a 'reasonable' person would have followed, this should assist you in your complaint.

Can I get a refund on an item I bought that I no longer like the colour or fit of?
No, the seller is within their rights to refuse a refund on items returned that are not faulty.

A shop may, depending on their policy, provide you with a credit note or refund you, but these options are purely at their discretion.

It is therefore advisable, before purchasing an item, to check the policy of the seller and the options available to you if you want to return it. Ask the seller to provide you with a small note in writing (signed and dated by the seller) of their policy regarding returns.

I was in town one day and I was in a hurry when buying a pair of trousers. I bought a size 14 (as that's what I normally wear). When I brought the trousers home they would not fit and when I compared them to my own trousers, they appeared like a size 12. The shop says they are not faulty.
First, it would always be advisable to try on clothing before purchasing due to the fact that sizes may vary from manufacturer to manufacturer. With reference to the Sale

of Goods and Supply of Services Act 1980, section 10(14) (2) states there is an implied condition that the goods are of merchantable quality. We would also have to consider if there was a defect clearly marked on the item, or one that a reasonable person would have found upon examination of the item. In addition, the Consumer Protection Act 2007 includes the consideration of whether a 'reasonable' person would have been misled to believe the item was labelled/sized correctly.

Therefore it would be advisable to return the item to the shop and seek a replacement (correct size). If the shop is unhelpful, you may wish to seek redress through the normal channels, i.e. written complaint and/or the Small Claims Court.

I was given a present by a friend for Christmas, but I already got the same present from someone else. Can I get a refund from the shop?
In this situation there is no fault with the item and therefore the shop is under no obligation to provide you with a refund. The shop may, at its discretion, provide you with a credit note or refund. It is advisable for anybody buying a present to check the policy of the shop in question regarding returns (non-faulty) before purchasing the item. It may be advisable not to purchase the item from that shop if in doubt. An alternative may be to ask for a 'gift receipt' when purchasing the item, which would allow for exchanges (subject to the shop policy).

Does a shop have a right to refuse the return of underwear or jewellery?
A shop can have a right to refuse the exchange of such items on grounds of personal hygiene. This right should

only apply to items that are returned on non-fault grounds. It is therefore advisable to ensure the item fits properly and that you are happy with it before you purchase.

This does not remove your statutory rights for a refund or replacement if the item is found to be faulty or not fit for the purpose required, or is not as described or as per the sample.

Purchasing Items in a Sale

If I return an item purchased before a sale, and there is a sale currently on in the shop, do I get a refund of the normal price or the sale price?
If there appears to be a fault (as per the Sale of Goods and Supply of Services Act 1980), and the seller has agreed to a refund, the refund price is the price the product was purchased at and not the sale price.

If I return an item during a sale and the company do not have a replacement item, what make and model should I receive?
If there appears to be a fault (as per the Sale of Goods and Supply of Services Act 1980), and the seller agrees to replace the item, the item should be the same model, or equal to or slightly better than the original model. The replacement model should not offer less (in operational function) than the original item.

If I buy an item in a sale, do I lose any of my rights?
No. In such cases, items are simply reduced in price but their quality and reliability should not be compromised. Your rights of remedy if a fault does occur are unaffected.

As a consumer you still have your full rights and options for remedy (the three Rs: Repair, Replace, Refund).

If an item is reduced for a specific purpose, i.e. a fault with the item, then the product should be marked 'seconds', or the consumer should be notified of such a fault before purchasing.

The shop where I bought a sale item had a notice saying 'No Refunds on Sale Items'. Can they do this?
No. It is not legal for a shop to display such notices, as they are trying to breach your statutory rights. Therefore, such notices are unenforceable by the seller. The notice only applies if you change your mind about an item and not if the item is faulty.

Credit Notes

I returned an item to a shop and the manager said that the shop only provides credit notes for returned items, not refunds. Is this true?
First, it is important to confirm that there was a fault with the product. If there was a fault, the Sale of Goods and Supply of Services Act 1980 applies and your remedies are the three Rs (Repair, Replace, Refund). The shop owner cannot refuse you your statutory rights and therefore a credit note does not have to be accepted by you, the consumer. If you only changed your mind about a product, e.g. its colour or design, then any exchange or credit note is at the discretion and policy of the shop.

Guarantees

I bought an item and the guarantee with it was for twelve months. I have now had it for thirteen months and a fault has occurred. Have I lost my legal rights?

No. A guarantee is simply an added bonus regarding the item. Section 15 of the Sale of Goods and Supply of Services Act 1980 states that a guarantee is that provided by a manufacturer or other supplier (other than a retailer) stating the manufacturer's policy should a fault occur after purchase. This guarantee does not remove the possibility of seeking redress for any fault that may occur with the item for up to the six years. There is still a duty of care on the seller, via the manufacturer, to ensure the product carries out its purpose for a reasonable period of time, and the seller is responsible to the buyer (section 17). The seller (in his/her own right) may provide additional guarantees, separate from those of the manufacturer. Rights under a guarantee do not limit the rights of the buyer to the guarantee only, and are provided in addition to their statutory rights under the Act (section 18). As a consumer, you may decide to take action against the manufacturer to fully perform their 'guarantee' and/or seek damages, in addition to seeking damages from the seller of the goods (section 19). The courts may force the manufacturer to carry out their guarantee to a reasonable satisfaction level within an agreed time frame (section 19). The old saying 'the more expensive the item, the greater expectation that the item will last' generally applies.

Guarantees must be legible, state the name and address of the supplier, state the duration of the guarantee and the process for making a claim under the guarantee, and what the supplier will do in relation to such complaint (section 16).

I purchased an electrical item in Northern Ireland, but it is now faulty. What is the situation regarding the guarantee? Can I make a small claims application?
A guarantee (as stated earlier) is simply an added bonus provided by the manufacturer, and does not affect your statutory rights. A manufacturer's guarantee may only be applicable in certain jurisdictions, i.e. the country in which the item was bought, subject to you residing in that jurisdiction. Therefore the manufacturer's guarantee may not be valid in this case if you reside in the Republic of Ireland and the item was purchased in Northern Ireland (check the small print). However, you are protected under the same quality and fit-for-purpose principles regarding goods and services under European law (Sale of Goods and Associated Guarantees Directive 99/44/EC). It would be advisable to complain directly (by phone and/or in writing) to the retailer from whom you purchased the item. If you continue to have difficulties you could seek assistance from the European Consumer Centre (www. eccireland.ie). In many cases, they can act as an intermediary in relation to disputes across borders.

In addition, since 1 January 2009 the new European-wide (excluding Denmark) Small Claims Procedure is in place. The same procedure applies and claims are submitted in the jurisdiction in which you reside. Applications under the European Small Claims Court process cannot be made online. However, applications in the Republic of Ireland can only be made online at www.courts.ie.

I purchased a new TV recently. The shop asked me if I want to buy an extra warranty for five years. Is this a con and if not what are the benefits?

Some shops sell different additional policies to provide extra cover over and above your statutory rights. Some policies also cover the same statutory rights as provided under law 'without quibble'. For example, some policies provide for 'accidental damage' which is not provided for under statutory legislation. This means if the items falls or is accidentally broken you can take it back to the shop and the item will be replaced or repaired under the policy without any fee or dispute (each policy is different; therefore, it is important for you to check all the small print before purchasing). This may be beneficial to you, depending on your situation, i.e. if there are small children or a higher risk of accidental damage and depending on the cost of the cover.

The policy may also cover areas already covered under law, i.e. a repair policy without dispute or complaint or the need to take a claim to the Small Claims Court (discussed later). As we are aware, all goods (excluding cars) are covered for a six-year period under consumer law (this may change in the future with the pending Consumer Rights Bill). These additional policies hopefully provide you with a dispute-free mechanism of returning damaged or broken items without the worry of having to complain. Therefore, for some people this may be worthwhile if you feel uncomfortable or not confident in asserting your rights. In conclusion, these additional protection policies are not compulsory, and can in some cases provide you with extra protection, but, as stated, you are already covered under law by the Repair, Replace or Refund protections and you have a right not to accept these additional policies if you do not wish to.

Misleading Advice from Shop Staff

I purchased tiles from a large renowned tile shop. I gave the salesperson the exact measurements of the floor. I followed his recommendation in relation to the number of boxes. After fitting the tiles I found I had three boxes over. The tile shop said they won't take them back. What can I do?

Section 10(14)(4) of the Sale of Goods and Supply of Services Act 1980 relies on the expertise of the salesperson in assessing the best requirements for the buyer. There may, understandably, be some surplus tiles, dependent on the number of boxes and taking into account some surplus for error/damage. Alternatively, it appears the salesperson may have made an incorrect judgement or calculation, depending on the details you provided to him. Therefore it is important to ensure:

- You have the exact measurements to give to the salesperson before purchasing tiles.
- You are fully informed (by the seller) of possible surplus.
- You know the return policy of the shop for surplus tiles.

If a dispute still arises, you may seek normal redress, i.e. formal complaints mechanism/Small Claims Court, for breach of section 10(14)(4).

I recently bought computer software from a PC shop. It is not compatible with my machine. The shop said that, as the packaging is open, there is no proof that the software has not been downloaded. They are not willing to give me a refund. What can I do?

There are a number of factors we must consider:

- Were you or should you have been reasonably aware the software would not be compatible?
- Did you ask the salesperson if the software would be compatible?

If the labelling led you to believe the software was compatible, your argument could be misleading advertising, or, under the new Consumer Protection Act 2007, that a reasonable person would have believed the item to be compatible. If this can be shown, you would seem to have a valid case that the item is not fit for the purpose required and should be refunded.

If you asked the salesperson and s/he advised you that the software would be compatible, then, under section 10(14)(4) of the Sale of Goods and Supply of Services Act 1980, you may have a valid case, i.e. the salesperson provided a 'fit for the purpose required' decision based on your needs.

Food Labelling

What is the situation regarding labelling and pricing of food items?
Food items sold loose or in bulk should display a unit price (per kilogramme or litre). Retailer and service providers in Ireland must show prices in euro and display the source, name of product and variety.

Pre-packed food items should contain information regarding the name, net quantity, best-before date, ingredients in weight order (decreasing), storage conditions, name and address of manufacturer, origin of product and alcoholic content (if greater than 1.2 per cent volume). If a product states a specific health claim (low in fat; low in sugar), nutritional information must be labelled on the product.

Food labelling is controlled by Environmental Health Officers in your local area (under the remit of the Health Service Executive (HSE)). Misleading advertising should be reported to the National Consumer Agency (www.nca. ie).

Pricing

Supposing I buy an item for €50 and the price is reduced six months later to €30. If the item purchased becomes faulty, what price refund should I receive? The seller tells me it is the new price. Is this true?

No. If the item you purchased becomes faulty and the agreed redress between you and the seller is a refund, the price refunded is the price the item was purchased at and the price stated on your receipt or proof of purchase, i.e. €50. If you simply change your mind, you may have to accept the new lower price, depending on the policy of the shop.

I bought an item one year ago and it was valued at €1,000. The item is now faulty and the seller has agreed to replace it, but the replacement item is now only sold for €400. Should I get a refund of the difference in price?

No. A refund for the difference in price, either now or even before a sale, is not applicable. The responsibility of the seller is to either repair, replace or refund the item, i.e. refund the price the item was purchased at.

In this case, as the item worked successfully for one year, such a fault may be minor and as the fault did not occur within the first six months, implying that it may not be a manufacturing fault, a replacement or repair to a suitable standard would be a suitable remedy.

I saw an item in a shop for €20, but when I got to the counter the correct price was €40. Do I have to pay the higher price?

It is important to note that if an item is incorrectly priced, the question raised is whether it was priced incorrectly by mistake or on purpose. When purchasing an item, the 'contract' for the purchase of the item takes place at the counter. The offer (price of item) and acceptance (by the consumer) with consideration (payment method) occurs at the counter. Therefore, if the seller informs you of an incorrectly priced item, they (the seller) have the right to offer you the product at the correct (higher) price, and you have the right to refuse to buy it. The shop may, at their discretion, honour the 'lower' price.

You, the consumer, have the right to refuse to accept the item at the new price and cancel the purchase. If the product is offered at the incorrect price (by the seller) and accepted (by the consumer) with consideration (payment) at the till, the transaction is complete.

If the item is incorrectly priced intentionally, you can make a complaint under misleading advertising, but this still does not give you the right to purchase the item at the incorrect price. The Consumer Protection Act 2007 increases penalties for retailers engaging in misleading advertising via the Unfair Commercial Practices Directive (Directive 2005/29/EC of the European Parliament and

of the Council of 11 May 2005). These new regulations treat misleading advertising and misleading an 'average' consumer as more serious offences than they were regarded as in the past. In such circumstances, action may include the consumer seeking compensation from the retailer.

I was in a chain store (owned by a large UK company) the other day. An item was priced at £30. What is the conversion rate to euro?
Although shops may have a sterling price on an item, a euro price must also be on the item. This euro price does not necessarily have to be the exact corresponding converted price from sterling (as per the relevant conversion rate); it can be higher or lower than the relevant sterling price.

The Consumer Protection Act 2007 gives the Minister for Enterprise, Jobs and Innovation powers to make regulations that require prices of certain products to be displayed in a certain manner. This power could force, as an example, UK chain stores to have prices in euro only, or force low-cost airlines to incorporate charges, fees and taxes into their advertised prices. If you have a complaint in relation to non- labelling of prices in euro, please contact the National Consumer Agency (www.nca.ie).

In addition, since 1 November 2008 (EU Regulation 1008/08), airlines are now required to include all taxes and charges in their published prices, as well as detailing the different elements that contribute to the price. Under this regulation, additional charges cannot now be imposed on passengers without their express consent.

Deliveries

I received a delivery of a suite of furniture the other day. It is not the same type or fabric that I ordered. What can I do?

If the item was purchased from a sample or display, the delivered item should be the same or equal to what you indicated on the day. As per the Sales of Goods and Supply of Services Act 1980 (section 10(15)), goods must correspond with any sample. There is also an implied condition that the goods should be free from any defect that would not have been apparent from viewing the sample.

It is also important, upon delivery or receipt of goods, to fully examine the goods. You must be given a reasonable time to do so even if the item has only been delivered (section 20(34)(1)). Only when you are happy the item conforms to the contract should you accept the delivery (section 20(35)).

If you feel the item does not correspond, you are within your rights to make a complaint to the seller of the goods.

I ordered a suite of furniture eighteen weeks ago and it has not yet arrived. The proposed delivery date was meant to be sixteen weeks. Can I do anything?

Under section 10 of the Sale of Goods and Supply of Services Act 1980 (from the Sale of Goods Act 1893, sections 11–15), if a contract of sale is subject to a condition, which was not completed by the seller, the buyer has two choices. S/he may decide either to cancel the contract (section 10(11)(2)), or to decide to treat it as a breach of warranty (therefore possibly seeking damages). It is important to examine the terms and conditions of the agreement, as there is a very important distinction between 'conditions' and 'warranties', and it is important to figure out what is fundamental to the agreement (even if it is called something else). What this means simply is that if the agreement to deliver a suite of furniture by an agreed date is broken, and this is a fundamental condition to the agreement, there may be valid grounds to cancel the order (and seek a refund) if the agreement is broken.

The value of 'damages' corresponds to the loss from the breach of warranty, or the difference between the value of the goods at time of delivery and the value they would have had if they answered to the warranty (section 21(53)(4)).

Purchasing Goods Privately

I am planning on buying a second-hand car privately. What should I look out for?
When buying a car second hand in a private transaction (not with an official seller) it is important to be aware that you are not covered under the Sale of Goods and Supply of Services Act 1980 and any dispute you may have in the future is a private (civil) dispute which could possibly require legal representation. In addition, there is no legislative redress for cars purchased through websites as they are not the seller, simply an agent to facilitate the sale.

The key items to check when purchasing a car in a private transaction are:

- **Check the valid owner of the car and if there is any finance on the car** – this can be checked for a small fee on www.cartell.ie. This check can also find out if the car was previously a taxi or was in a road accident/s.

- **Ensure the name on the documentation complies with photo ID** – it is essential the person selling the car is the actual owner of the car.
- **Purchase the car from the vehicle owner's address** – be aware of purchasing a car in a public place. Don't assume that the house the car is parked outside is the owner's house.
- **Pay by bank draft** – it is important that payment is made by bank draft or cheque and not by cash.
- **Vehicle history/check** – ensure the vehicle is independently checked by a mechanic and copies of all service history is available. This service is available from www.aaireland.ie or www.cartell.ie for agreed rates.

The purchase of a second-hand car is one of the biggest financial decisions to make. Don't be rushed into any sale. If the offer sounds too good to be true, then it probably is. As always, 'Let the buyer beware'.

SUMMARY CHECKLIST: Purchasing Goods, Pricing and Returning Items

Purchasing Goods

Have you checked the item in the shop (to a reasonable level)?	☐
Is the item marked 'faulty/seconds'?	☐
If buying an item and you get advice/guidance from a shop assistant on the choice, purpose or number of items required, make sure you get the person's name.	☐
If there is a manufacturer's guarantee, what period does it cover and what jurisdiction?	☐
If buying clothes, try on the item before leaving the shop.	☐
If buying a present, check the shop policy on returns, and if there is a time limit for exchange (change of mind).	☐

Pricing

Make sure the item is priced in euro. ☐

If you get to the counter and the incorrect price is charged, you can decide to cancel, or the shop may, at their discretion, honour the price. ☐

If items are not priced, or incorrectly priced, report it to the National Consumer Agency. ☐

Returning Items

What is the policy of the shop in relation to refunds? Are refunds given at the time of return or by post? ☐

Always keep your proof of purchase, e.g. receipt, cheque stub, etc. ☐

If the fault is within the first six months, the item should be replaced without quibble. ☐

If there is a fault, what is the procedure, and how long should it take to be repaired? Will the shop provide a temporary replacement? ☐

In making a complaint be assertive but not aggressive. ☐

Do not tamper, open or use the goods for purposes other than those stated. Such action will remove the possibility of redress. ☐

As soon as you become aware of any fault, act promptly and return the item to the shop. ☐

Were you misled regarding your purchase? Would a 'reasonable' person have been misled? You may have a valid case. ☐

Services

Does the Sale of Goods and Supply of Services Act 1980 cover services and service providers?

Yes, the Sale of Goods Act also covers the supply of services. Therefore the Act also covers service providers, i.e. tradespeople, fitters, etc.

In seeking tradesmen or fitters, ensure they are aware of the following conditions of the Act (section 39):

- The supplier has the necessary skill to complete the service.
- The supplier will supply the service with due skill, care and diligence.
- The materials used will be sound and reasonably fit for the purpose required.
- Goods supplied under the agreement will be of merchantable quality.

I left my suede jacket in to be dry cleaned. When I got the jacket back it was damaged. What can I do?
The dry cleaners, as experts in this area, must act with due skill, care and diligence, and use correct materials that are of merchantable quality. Therefore if a problem arises in relation to damage, the service provider must show compliance with all of the above. The consumer, therefore, has the right to seek redress under the three Rs – Repair, Replace or Refund. As it may be impossible for the jacket to be repaired, the consumer may seek a replacement or refund. It would therefore be advisable to ensure you put your complaint in writing and to keep a copy. If no agreeable outcome is achieved, you may have to take action in the Small Claims Court.

The dry cleaner said it was the fault of the seller of the jacket, as the instructions were incorrect. What should I do?
It may be advisable to return the item to the shop you purchased the item from, due to the fact that the washing

instructions were complied with and the fault still occurred. As stated earlier, proof of purchase is required. Alternatively, the service provider will be required to prove compliance with due skill, care and professional diligence.

It may be worthwhile taking an action against both the retailer and the service provider. If the matter progresses to the Small Claims Court, the full facts of the situation will have to be investigated: whether there is contributory negligence on either/both sides, and what proportion is attributed to either.

I am with a large telecoms company. If you don't pay your bill by direct debit, they charge you an extra fee. Can they do this?

No. Under the Consumer Protection Act 2007 (section 48(3)) the practice of charging customers more for different methods of payment, e.g. cash, credit card or direct debit, is prohibited. The one exception is if the only method of payment is by credit card, or if the charge applies to all methods of payment but the price includes the surcharge. A trader who breaches subsection (3) commits an offence and is liable on summary conviction to a fine of €3,000 or imprisonment for a term not exceeding six months, or both (section 79(a)). For any subsequent summary conviction for the same offence, a trader is liable for a fine of €5,000 or imprisonment for a term not exceeding twelve months, or both. In addition, section 81 can impose payment of compensation to consumers for loss or damage. Prosecution may be commenced at any time within two years of the date of the alleged offence (section 76).

I had a dispute with a tradesman and he did not finish the job. What can I do?
It is advisable before seeking the services of tradespeople that you examine recognised trade bodies (if applicable) to seek registered members (i.e. those with skilled services), or alternatively to check references of previous work completed by such tradesmen (i.e. due skill, care and diligence). It is also important to set out a written agreement before the work commences covering the exact nature of the work, materials required (merchantable quality/fit for the purpose), payment and, ideally, dispute resolution. If, having tried to discuss your complaint with the tradesperson, the dispute is not resolved, i.e. they will not return and complete the work to a specified standard, it may be advisable to send a formal complaint to them and keep a copy.

I joined a gym recently, and it appears I am 'locked into' a contract and they require three months' notice to cancel it. What can I do?
It is extremely important when signing up for a service that you fully check the small print in the contract. It is important to be completely aware of the contract period, notice period and what the procedure is to cancel. If you have complied with the proper notice, and the gym continues to deduct payments by direct debit, it is important to notify both the gym and the bank. Generally direct debits can only be cancelled by the service provider. If payments are still being deducted, you should submit your complaint in writing and, if required, submit a claim to the Small Claims Court. If you were misled as part of the selling process, or if you felt the terms of the contract were unfair and unreasonable, it is advisable to contact

the National Consumer Agency (www.nca.ie) to report the incident.

Unfair commercial practices are those that are in breach of 'good faith' or of the standards of skill and care that would cause a reasonable and average person to be misled or be unable or impaired from making an 'informed decision' in availing of a product or service. The European Court of Justice interprets the 'average consumer' as 'reasonably well informed and reasonably observant and circumspect, taking into account social cultural and linguistic factors'. Misleading commercial practices occur when false information misleads or deceives a consumer regarding a product or service (sections 41–56 of the Consumer Protection Act 2007). Aggressive commercial practices are applicable if harassment, coercion or undue influence impair the average consumer's freedom of choice or make them carry out a transaction they would not normally make (section 53). In 2011 the National Consumer Agency sought consultation from the public to develop guidelines to avoid unfair terms in consumer contracts.

What is the legal situation in relation to 'pyramid schemes'?
Under the Consumer Protection Act 2007, it is an offence to establish, operate, promote, participate or entice another person to take part in a pyramid scheme. The penalties for such an offence are a fine of up to €150,000 and a prison term of five years. This prevents people who have paid into such schemes from seeking any legal means to recover such payments.

The Act also prevents aggressive commercial behaviour that prevents consumers (through harassment or undue influence) from freely making choices. The Act introduces more transparency in relation to consumers having full view of the pricing of items. It advances punishments for retailers who mislead a 'reasonable' consumer, such as fixed penalties, 'naming and shaming', and possible award of damages to consumers.

SUMMARY CHECKLIST: Services

Is the tradesperson/service provider qualified and experienced in his/her area of expertise? □

Will the tradesperson/service provider act with due care, skill and diligence? □

Are the materials to be used correct for the job required, and of merchantable quality? □

Do you have experience of the person's previous work, e.g. have they been referred to you by someone else? □

Is there a written agreement regarding the price, agreed work and time frame for completion? Will there be a valid receipt for payment? □

Is there an agreement as to how payment should be made, i.e. before, during or after completion? □

Do they have cover for liability or vicarious liability, i.e. damage to another party when on site? Under EU law it may become a requirement for homeowners to have 'practical' health and safety measures in place to protect the service provider and prevent the possibility of being sued. □

Is the work guaranteed for a period of time, durability or purpose? □

Do you have a registered address or landline number and not a PO Box number or mobile phone number only, for the service provider? □

Is the fitter or tradesperson registered with a representation body, registered for tax and compliant with company law? □

Holidays and Travel

Passports

Who needs a passport? How much does it cost and what do I need in order to apply for one?
Since October 2004, all children, regardless of age, must obtain an individual Irish passport in their own name. However, parents' passports issued before 1 October 2004 on which children have been included remain valid and do not need to be replaced. Children who are included on a parent's passport issued before 1 October 2004 may continue to travel to most countries up to their sixteenth birthday along with that parent, provided the passport is still valid. The countries that are exceptions include the Czech Republic, Estonia and the US.

The fee for a standard ten-year passport is €80. A replacement passport is the same price as a new passport (€80). A five-year passport for children from three to seventeen years of age costs €26.50, and a three-year passport for children aged under three years is €16. An Post has a passport express service which guarantees you will get your passport within ten working days. The cost of this service is €8.50 per application or a family rate of €14.50 (for four family applications in one envelope). The public counters and out of hours services should only be used by those who have a necessity to travel for reasons of family emergency, i.e. travel is necessitated by the death, illness or welfare of a family member. There is an extra fee of €55 per adult and €30 per child and passports will be processed within three working days. The fee for normal passports applications in person or by normal/registered post is an extra €15. Normal postal applications take at least eight weeks and public office applications take approximately two weeks.

Since January 2011 first-time adult applications require:

- Birth Certificate.
- Marriage Certificate.
- Four photos – two signed and witnessed.
- Photo ID – copy of driver's licence, student card, work ID, etc.
- Evidence showing use of your name, e.g. payslips, bank statements, etc.
- Residency address proof – utility bill etc.

Who can sign a passport application and what should I do if I plan to take my grandchild or other people's children on holiday with me?

For married couples and joint legal guardians, both parents must sign the passport application form. If one of the legal guardians refuses to sign the application, you will have to seek the intervention of the District Court for assistance. For single parents where the father is not a legal guardian only the mother's signature is required.

It is also important to note if you are a grandparent or travelling with children who are not your own, it is advisable to get written authorisation from the parent(s) prior to departing. It may even be advisable to get a legal affidavit signed by the parent(s) before you travel. Alternatively, you may wish to seek legal opinion prior to travel to ensure there are no difficulties along the way.

Air Travel

What are my rights when I fly within Europe?

Under EC Regulation 261/2004, you are protected if you travel within Europe and from outside Europe to a

European destination, assuming you are travelling on an air carrier registered within the EU. Passengers travelling free of charge or at a reduced rate not available to the public are not covered by this Regulation. In addition, the Regulation only covers passengers who have a confirmed reservation and have presented for check-in no later than forty-five minutes before the expected departed time.

I booked a flight with a low-budget airline. Where do I get information about my rights?
Your rights as a passenger should and must be displayed at the check-in desk (Article 14). If your flight is delayed for over two hours or you are denied boarding, you must be given a written note stating your entitlements. For blind or visually impaired people, information must be provided by alternative means.

Can I claim compensation for cancelled flights due to bad weather or volcanic ash? What are my rights in relation to cancelled flights?
No, unfortunately 'metrological conditions incompatible with the operation of the flight concerned' prevents you from seeking financial compensation. However, under the Regulation you are entitled to reasonable meals and refreshments in relation to the waiting time, two phone calls or emails and, if your flight is delayed until the following day, hotel accommodation and transport to and from the airport as necessary and as required. In addition, you are entitled to reimbursement (covering the cost of hotel accommodation and associated costs) within seven days by cash, electronic bank transfer or travel vouchers for the cost of the flight and/or connecting flights and, if relevant, a return flight to the first point of departure. Alternatively you could accept

re-routing at a later date at the passengers' convenience subject to seat availability. It is essential that you keep a copy of all associated costs and receipts and submit receipts to the airline as quickly as possible. It may be advisable to send your receipts by registered post to guarantee delivery.

For the airline to avoid paying compensation they must provide you with two weeks' notice of rerouting or cancellation in advance of the original departure date. They must also provide you with an alternative flight or full refund of the price of your ticket. If you have been given between seven and fourteen days' notice in advance of the original departure date, you must be given an alternative flight departing no more than two hours before your scheduled flight and arriving no later than four hours after your previous scheduled time. Alternatively, they must provide you with a refund of the full ticket price. For a cancellation with less than seven days' notice, the airline must provide you with a flight departing no more than one hour before your previous scheduled flight and arriving no more than two hours later than your previous scheduled time, or a full refund of the ticket price.

What if this re-routing is to an alternative airport?
The air carrier is liable for the cost of transferring the passenger from the alternative arrival airport to the original arrival airport, or to an alternative airport, in agreement with the passenger.

Can people on package holidays claim this compensation for rerouting or cancellation of flights?
Yes, people on package holidays can claim the above compensation but only if the flight is cancelled and not if their package is cancelled.

If your package is cancelled, you are entitled to an equivalent holiday of superior quality, a lower grade holiday with partial refund or a full refund. The organiser can also cancel package holidays due to 'acts of God', and in those circumstances no compensation is due.

What about my travel insurance. Am I covered?
It is important to check the small print of your insurance cover. If your policy covers 'acts of God' and the provider will not pay, you will have to put your complaint in writing and, if unresolved, make a complaint to the Financial Regulator.

What if my flight is simply delayed?
If the delay is more than two hours (for flight distances 1,500km or less), three hours (1,500–3,500km) and four hours (greater than 3,500km), you are entitled to reasonable meals and refreshments and two free phone calls. If the flight is delayed until the following day, you are entitled to overnight accommodation and transport to and from your accommodation to the airport and two free calls. If the delay is greater than five hours, you are entitled to reimbursement of the cost of the flight and a return flight or re-routed flight. In a recent European Court of Justice case, it was determined that compensation for delays should be paid where the delay exceeds three hours.

When can you claim compensation?
Compensation can be claimed when you have been denied boarding or your flight was cancelled (including for reasons of technical faults). Operators can limit liability if they can prove all reasonable steps were taken to avoid such delays. The European Court of Justice has ruled that the

cancellation of a flight due to a 'technical fault' is not an 'extraordinary circumstance' and therefore compensation should be awarded to passengers in these circumstances. The amount is €250 (for flights distances 1,500km or less), €400 (1,500–3,500km) and €600 (for flights greater than 3,500km). If you are re-routed and your delay is less than two hours (for flight distances 1,500km or less), three hours (for flights 1,500–3,500km) and four hours (greater than 3,500km), the compensation may be reduced by 50 per cent. The greater circle route method is the technically defined measurement for the provision of compensation.

What are my rights if I have been denied boarding?

If you have been denied boarding due to overbooking, the following should take place (Article 4):

- People may volunteer not to board a flight – these passengers may seek compensation and/or alternative flights or refunds. Arrangements will be made between the volunteer and the airline as to the compensatory package.
- If insufficient volunteers come forward, people may be selected not to board – these passengers can claim immediate entitlement to compensation from €250 to €600, depending on the duration of the flight (see above) (Article 7). Alternatively, you may be provided with a choice of refund (and a free flight back to your point of departure) or transport to your final destination (Article 8), and/or overnight accommodation, a free meal, refreshments, free transport to and from the place of accommodation (to and from the airport) and two telephone calls, where it becomes necessary (Article 9). People with reduced mobility or special needs should be prioritised (Article 11).

Do I have any other rights regarding travel, injury or lost luggage?

- In the case of death or injury – compensation may be sought under the Montreal Convention 1999 and EU Regulation 889/2002. There is no financial limit in the event of death or injury. Damages up to 113,100 Special Drawing Rights (SDR), i.e. €134,090.23, is generally uncontested by airlines. The SDR rate is 1.185590 in 2012 and will be 1.189120 in 2013 (the SDR is a mix of currency values established by the IMF; more details can be found at www.imf.org). If you are injured or killed, 16,000 SDR (€18,969.44) must be paid within fifteen days to cover immediate needs. Claims must be made within two years of death.
- Downgrades (Article 10) – refunds of between 30 per cent of the ticket price (for flights less than 1,500km), 50 per cent (flights between 1,500 and 3,500km) and 75 per cent (flights over 3,500km) can be offered for downgrades.
- Lost, damaged or delayed baggage – all reports must be made in writing as soon as practicably possible. The value of such baggage is calculated under SDR. The value of lost, destroyed or damaged luggage is calculated at a set rate of 1,131 SDR (€1,340.90) (checked baggage). Luggage is classed as lost if it does not arrive within 21 days of the scheduled arrival date. The airline is only liable for unchecked baggage if it was at fault. Complaints must be made within 7 days if the luggage is damaged or destroyed or within 28 days if it is lost or delayed. It is advisable to keep your luggage labels safe. If your luggage does not arrive or is damaged at the airport, you should complete a Property Irregularity Report (PIR) containing all your relevant details (flight, contact details, etc). You will be given a copy for your records. All complaints thereafter should be put in writing, with as much evidence as possible, i.e.

photographs of damaged luggage, itinerary of items, etc. As is best practice, letters should be sent by registered post for proof of receipt. Court action for claims must be submitted within two years of the initial scheduled arrival date. It is important, therefore, to insure specified or special items and/or have them sent separately, and to submit claims under your travel insurance in addition. Since 17 February 2005, the Commission for Aviation Regulation is responsible for enforcing compensation only upon non-resolution with your airline directly. Further information can be found on the European Commission website http://ec.europa. eu/transport/passenger-rights/ or on www.flightrights. ie (provided by the Commission for Aviation Regulation).

In addition, since October 2011 the European Communities (Communication of Passenger Data) Regulations 2011 transposed Council Directive 2004/82/EC of 29 April, 2004 on the obligation of air carriers to communicate passenger data in advance to Irish Immigration authorities for the purposes of improving border control and combating illegal immigration for all flights from outside the EU. This information will be transmitted after the completion of flight check-in. The data must be destroyed after 24 hours of arrival. Information contained will include nationality, names, date of birth, port of arrival and departure, and arrival times. If a 'person of concern' is found on the lists, i.e. has committed or is suspected of committing an offence, information can be held for up to three years. Ireland and the UK also signed an agreement preserving the Common Travel Area, with effect since December 2011. As part of the agreement, information will also be shared regarding visa applications for the purpose of reducing illegal immigration.

Travelling to and from the US

I am planning to go shopping in New York. My friends tell me there are loads of bargains. Is there any restriction on the amount or value of goods I can bring home?
Yes, when returning from non-EU countries the combined value of goods should not exceed €175 (gifts, souvenirs, clothing and beer), excluding duty-free limits. If the value of the goods is in excess of the threshold, you must use the Red Channel at customs. People travelling together cannot pool their individual allowances to buy goods. Goods for commercial use must be declared at customs.

I am planning on going to the US on holidays. Do I need a visa?
The only situation where you require a visa to enter the US on holidays is if your passport is not a machine-readable passport. Passports issued prior to 26 June 2005 are not machine-readable. Since October 2004, all persons (including children) require their own passport to travel to the US.

As of 12 January 2009, you need to register online through the Electronic System for Travel Authorisation (ESTA) (https://esta. cbp.dhs.gov/esta/) at least 72 hours before travelling to the US.

Package Holidays

What are my rights in a dispute regarding a package holiday?
It is important to distinguish whether a dispute is regarding delays on flights (discussed earlier) or a package holiday (under the Package Holiday and Travel Trade Act 1995).

A package holiday combines the costs of transport, accommodation, specific facilities and tours (this

41

combination must make up a significant proportion of the holiday) and applies regardless of whether the items are paid for separately or are bundle priced (all-in). Individual requirements (e.g. sea-view room, second floor, etc.) are excluded.

A written contract must be given to all consumers in advance (except where departure is less than fourteen days from the time of booking) giving details of the booking. Problems may arise before, during or after a holiday takes place. It is important to clearly identify and report your complaint as soon as it is practicably possible.

Disputes may be taken to the Small Claims Court (maximum threshold for compensation is €2,000) if they are not resolved via the operator's dispute resolution procedure.

I book my holidays online and my flights and accommodation separately. Am I covered if anything goes wrong?
At present your holiday is not defined as a package holiday and therefore you would have to deal with any disputes according to your air travel rights and/or EU consumer rights (if within the EU) under the new European Small Claims Court. Due to changes in consumer travel, the EU Commission is considering reviewing the Package Travel Directive and sought submissions from the public between November 2009 and February 2010. Discussions also took place in April 2010 at the Albert Borschette Conference Centre in Brussels to further discuss a review.

I am going on holidays shortly. I am worried about the number of travel agencies going bust. What happens if this occurs while I am on holiday? How will I get home?
It is important that you book your travel package with a licensed and bonded travel agent. Therefore, if any

problems arise prior to or during your holidays there is a fund in place that will organise return flights if you are stranded abroad, and will refund you if you have not yet travelled. If you organised your holiday yourself, book-ing flights and hotels separately, there is no similar bond or protection in place. According to section 14 of the Sale of Goods and Supply of Services Act 1980, a finance house (credit card company) and seller are jointly and severally liable to the buyer for any breach of the contract of sale if problems arise. A list of licensed travel agents and tour operators can be found on www.aviationreg.ie. Claim forms (to seek a refund of payment or to cover outstanding charges for hotels or flights) can also be downloaded from the above website. The scheme only covers flights departing from the Republic of Ireland. The scheme is administered by the Commission for Aviation Regulation.

I have a gift voucher for a tour operator. If the tour oper-ator goes bust, can this be reclaimed from the Aviation Regulator?
Unless the voucher has been used for full or part payment for specific travel from the Republic of Ireland, unfortu-nately you are not entitled to protection under the bond protection in this case. A refund may be sought from the finance house or credit card company (section 14 of the Sale of Goods and Supply of Services Act 1980) or a refund may be sought from the liquidator (as an outstanding creditor). In this case, you may receive full, partial or, unfortunately, no payment, depending on how much money is left after liquidation.

Driving Abroad/Car Rental

I am planning on driving my car abroad. What should I take in terms of documentation?

Obviously make sure you take your driving licence and it is still valid. If travelling outside the European Economic Area (EEA), you may be required to have an international driving licence permit in addition to your licence. You will also need to check your car insurance to see if you are covered abroad.

An international driving permit is available to Irish residents who have a full driving licence. EU citizens who have a driving licence from their own country and reside in Ireland can get a driving permit from Ireland. Your driving licence must have at least a further six months remaining.

A one-year permit costs €10. No new driving test is required. The application is issued by the AA. A completed form, photo and fee are required. An additional €5 is required for postal applications. For EU citizens, a utility bill is required.

I am planning on renting a car. How can I prepare?

Generally the contract for car hires starts at the time of 'pick-up'. Check what the policy is regarding fuel. Will the car have a full tank when you pick it up? Do you have to leave it back with a full tank? Are there costs per mile/km travelled and to where should you return the car?

Thoroughly inspect the car before renting and if there are damages before you rent make a note of them and inform the provider. Take pictures both before and after the car rental.

Be aware of all the terms and conditions. You are liable if you sign a document so beware of the small print.

So what are the main checklist items for renting a car?

- **Tyres** – ensure that they are inflated and in good repair. Remember to check the spare tyre as well.
- **Tools** – check that, at the very least, there is a jack and a wrench to replace a tyre should you get a puncture. Also, make sure that you have all the necessary safety equipment needed for the area in which you are travelling.
- **Fuel** – ask if the car runs on petrol or diesel; you may be liable for putting in the wrong type of fuel. Generally, you need to refill the vehicle before you return it so ensure that you have a full tank of petrol when you start.
- **Lights** – ensure that your lights are all working adequately. This includes indicators, brake lights and fog lights.
- **Windscreen** – even the smallest flaw on a windscreen can lead to a large crack, so give the windscreen a thorough check and ask for any flaws to be repaired. Make sure that the wiper blades and the windscreen wash system is working adequately.
- **Insurance** – check that you have the appropriate insurance. If you and another person will be driving, check that you are both insured. If you are offered reductions in price for not having particular cover (such as collision damage waiver – CDW), think carefully about what this means before waiving this cover. Also, clarify how this discount works – for example, do you need to leave a deposit in case you cause damage to the car in a collision.
- **Check the car** – even if collecting the car at night time, ask for a torch and take photos before and after.
- **Rates** – different rates apply to different car rental agreements from different companies. Shop around for the

best deals, either on the internet or by telephoning car rental companies. The cheapest is not always the best!

- **Breakdown Service** – does the policy have a breakdown service and contact details?
- **Toll Fees** – generally toll fees are now paid by the rental company, so be advised that a later fee may be deducted from your credit or debit card for this.

Is there a body in charge of car rentals to whom complaints can be made?

The Car Rental Council of Ireland (www.carrentalcouncil.ie) is the body in charge. A list of members are on the site. All members have agreed to accept the rules and requirements.

Complaints should be made in writing to the rental company directly. If you have had no response, you should complain in writing to the Car Rental Council (if they are a member). In the UK, the body is British Vehicle and Rental Association (www.bvrla.co.uk).

Complaints can also be made under the Unfair Commercial Practices Directive, which prohibits unfair terms, misleading action, omissions and aggressive practices, and harassment and undue influence. The European Consumer Centre can assist with issues across Europe; in addition, the Small Claims Court is now European wide (excluding Denmark). Claims can only be submitted in paper form and in the jurisdiction in which you live. Each claim costs €25.

Sickness and Death Abroad

How can I protect myself for sickness abroad and do I need travel insurance?
The European Health Insurance Card (EHIC) replaced the E111 form. The card entitles you to the basic state-funded health care in the country in which you are staying on holidays. The level of care provided is defined as *'benefits granted with a view to preventing an insured person from being forced to return home to their home member state and enabling them to continue their temporary stay in another member state under safe medical conditions'* (Decision 194 of 2003). Countries covered consist of the 27 EEA states, together with Iceland, Norway and Liechtenstein. Every member of the family will require their own card. You can apply online at www.ehic.ie. There is no fee for the card.

Travel insurance is optional. The EHIC will not cover any of the costs involved in transporting you back to Ireland. Travel insurance provides extra cover, including for lost baggage, personal injury and transport home. Policies can vary on price and content. You do not have to accept the travel insurance provided by your travel agent.

What should I do if there are major problems abroad or a sudden bereavement?
If you are in urgent need of assistance, contact the Irish embassy/consulate. If one is not available, you can seek assistance from an EU embassy. Embassies can assist with lost/stolen passports, issues of crime, imprisonment, or a death abroad where a body has to be returned home. Repatriation may take place in exceptional circumstances at the discretion of the Department of Foreign Affairs. This

may involve an agreement to repay the costs on return. For more information, check www.dfa.ie.

SUMMARY CHECKLIST: Holidays and Travel

Keep a copy of the brochure, and/or description of the holiday, as you may need to rely on the facts presented to you at a later date. ☐

Ensure all the correct details are recorded on your application form, i.e. correct names (as per passports), requirements, prices, deposits paid and travel arrangements. ☐

Do you need a visa, or machine-readable passports? (If visiting the US, machine-readable passports are required since June 2005. Alternatively a visa is required.) It is your responsibility to investigate. ☐

Since October 2004, all minors are required to have their own passports. Minors already on their parent's passports may travel with their parents up to their sixteenth birthday. ☐

Ensure to read all the small print on the application form before signing/approving. ☐

Price changes - changes are allowable but only under specific conditions, e.g. oil price increase or decrease. ☐

No price increases may be made within 21 days of departure. ☐

Altered travel arrangements - the operator should inform the consumer as soon as possible regarding such changes, and the consumer should be given the option of an alternative at equal or greater value, partial refund or full refund. ☐

Cancellation time frames - it is important for the consumer to be fully aware of the time periods for cancellation and/or percentage rebates. ☐

Ensure you have an European Health Insurance Card (EHIC) if travelling in Europe. Available free of charge from www. ehic.ie. ☐

Be aware of the terms and conditions of your travel insurance. You are not obliged to take the insurance provided by your travel agent. If you are pregnant, inform your travel agency or tour operator in advance. ☐

Transfer of bookings - are there any clauses and/or extra costs in relation to changes in your booking or administrative changes/mistakes? ☐

Bonded - ensure the tour operator is bonded, i.e. licensed under the Tour Operator and Travel Agents Act 1982, in the event of financial difficulties. To check the list of 'bonded' operators, see www.aviationreg.ie. ☐

Disputes – what is the specific dispute resolution procedure and time frame for making complaints abroad, or upon return home? ☐

Missing, delayed or damaged luggage should be reported directly to your airline as soon as practicable, i.e. after landing. Ensure you receive a receipt of acknowledgement. ☐

Be aware of the maximum allowances for lost or damaged luggage. It may be advisable not to take expensive/high value goods without additional insurance cover. ☐

Ensure you are aware of your rights in relation to delays, over-bookings and cancellations, and ensure you receive your entitlements. Complaints in relation to flights (non-package holidays), if not resolved by your airline, should be reported to the Aviation Regulator (www.flightrights.ie). ☐

Report any faults to your representative (whilst on holiday) as soon as you become aware of them. ☐

Be sure to receive a valid receipted log report from your travel representative whilst on holidays. ☐

Be aware of customs/duty-free limits, if applicable. ☐

Take photos as needed to support your claim, if you have a dispute and will be taking action. ☐

Be sure to formally complain to your travel agent (or organisation with whom you had your contract) within the agreed time frame upon return. ☐

It would be advisable to send your complaint in writing by registered post with all supporting details and documentation clearly stating your requested resolution. ☐

If no response is received, submit your claim to the Small Claims Court (maximum claim €2,000). ☐

Consumer Rights – General

*EU Consumer Rights Directive and Pending Consumer
Rights Act 2012*

*I have heard the rights of consumers may be changing in
the future. What will this mean and will it improve my
rights?*
The European Commission simplified three existing
Directives (the Distance Selling Directive (Directive 97/7/
EC), the Consumer Sale of Goods and Guarantees Directive
(Directive 1999/44/EC) and the Unfair Contract Terms
Directive (Directive 93/13/EEC)) into the new Consumer
Rights Directive which came into effect in June 2011 and
was adopted by the Council of the European Union on
the 10 October 2011. It has been fully operational since 13
December 2011. This now requires traders to:

- Provide consumers with clear information on the product or service in advance of purchase.
- Be responsible for any damage of goods in transit up to the time the consumer takes possession.
- Provide an EU-wide fourteen-day cooling-off period from the date of receipt (this may be extended to a year if the seller did not clearly inform the customer). Refunds must be received with fourteen days, including the cost of delivery. If a trader does not clearly inform the customer of the return charges and estimated costs of delivery in advance of the purchase, the trader will have to pay for the return charges themselves.
- Ban pre-ticked boxes (and additional implicit costs incurred).
- Protect online auction sites (discussed earlier).

- Ensure a 30-day delivery. If the delivery is late or does not occur, the consumer must receive a refund within seven days.
- Provide an EU-wide model withdrawal form if consumers wish to change their mind and withdraw from distance/doorstep contracts.
- Provide better consumer rights in relation to digital products, i.e. compatibility and copying content prior to downloading.
- Ensure the removal of credit card or payment fees that exceed the actual cost borne by the trader. In addition, traders who provide telephone hotlines to allow consumers to contact them will not be able to charge more than the basic telephone rate for the calls.

In addition, certain small businesspeople and craftspeople may be entitled to urgent repairs and maintenance up to the value of €200 regarding the provision or non-provision of some information requests. There will be no right of withdrawal for urgent repairs and maintenance.

This Directive now needs to be transposed into Irish Law by 13 December 2013 (to be known as the Consumer Rights Bill) before it can be become law. Some changes may be implemented by way of a statutory instrument in 2012, i.e. credit card and additional payment fees, pre-ticked boxes and changes in relation to 'small' print. In addition, the Minister for Jobs, Enterprise and Innovation proposes to add the following changes to the areas already protected under the EU Consumer Rights Directive:

- That 'small' print be of a minimum mandatory size and font and in black.
- That a receipt is issued for all consumer transactions.

- That consumers have the right to reject faulty goods within 30 days (this replaces the existing misinterpreted and misunderstood rules).
- The increase in guarantees and quality of goods (removing the possibility of contractual exclusions), i.e. a change from 'merchantable' quality to 'satisfactory' quality. This change will focus on what a 'reasonable' person would expect in relation to description, price, safety, durability and other factors.
- To comply with the United Nations Convention on Contracts for International Sale of Goods.

In addition, a new Alternative Dispute Resolution (ADR) is being proposed by the European Commission (November 2011) to eliminate the need to go to court for consumer complaints. This would include use of existing ADR organisations in each member state and a European-wide consumer disputes mechanism via a new European-wide online platform to solve contractual disputes within 30 days.

Shopping Online

I bought some goods on eBay and when I received them they were faulty. What are my rights?
Unfortunately goods bought in online auctions, or as part of a private transaction (one-to-one) are not covered under the European Directive on Distance Selling (as they are not between a consumer and supplier of goods and services), and therefore any dispute between two parties is a civil dispute. Some providers have their own customer service policies or Code of Conduct in place, but these are not statutory protections under law and are simply 'best practice'.

The new EU Consumer Rights Directive *(discussed later)* now implements a fourteen-day period to change your mind for goods bought through online auctions, e.g. eBay, but only if bought from a professional seller.

I am concerned about shopping online. Am I protected inside and outside the EU?

Specific legislation (Electronic Commerce Act 2000, which gives online details the same legal status as written details) and directives (EU Directive on Distance Selling SI 207/2001, which covers cooling-off periods and communication between people not in each other's physical presence) have been set up to protect online shoppers (including purchases by telephone) and to put them in the same or a slightly better position than if they were dealing with a 'normal, physical' retailer. Under section 3 of the EU Directive on Distance Selling, a 'distance contract' is one between a supplier and a consumer in relation to goods and services. A distance contract is not applicable if made by automated calling machines or by fax (unless prior consent is given).

Under the Directive, the cooling-off period is seven days, starting with day one (date of receipt of item), during which time you can cancel without reason and without penalties (other than possible return postage charges). For services, day one starts when the contract is completed or documents are received. In some cases the cooling-off period may be extended to three months. Certain goods (newspapers, magazines, and audio, video and software equipment where the seal has been broken) cannot be cancelled. If the product is unavailable, the consumer may decide to accept an alternative item, subject to an 'opt-out' without penalty, if they decide to cancel. Refunds must be repaid within 30 days. Financial services, contracts for the sale of land or auctions, and food and drink are excluded from the remit of the Directive on Distance Selling. Other transactions not applicable are the provision of accommodation, transport and leisure services on the grounds that such provision is supplied according to a specified date and time.

If you have a dispute in relation to the seller, and have been unsuccessful in dealing with them, and they are within the EU (including the UK), you may wish to seek assistance from the European Consumer Centre (www. eccireland.ie). Disputes with sellers outside of the EU are not protected under the above legislation.

SUMMARY CHECKLIST: Shopping Online

Make sure you are aware of the name, address and physical location, and contact details of the seller (section 5 of the Directive on Distance Selling). ☐

Is the 'cooling-off' period longer than seven days (section 6 of the Directive on Distance Selling; fourteen days under the new Consumer Rights Directive)? ☐

What is the total price charged and in what currency? ☐

Is VAT applicable and/or a customs duty? ☐

Who is responsible for charges, i.e. delivery charges/custom duty? The new EU Consumer Rights Directive imposes new responsibilities on traders to fully explain the return costs. ☐

Can the item be imported? ☐

What is the procedure in relation to the order processing, i.e. order confirmation, order tracking and time frame for delivery? ☐

Do you have a receipt? (Confirmation is required under sections 4 and 5 of the Directive on Distance Selling.) (You may wish to print out the confirmation page.) ☐

What is the procedure for non-delivery? Normally, if the contract or agreement exceeds 30 days (section 9(1) of the Directive on Distance Selling) without completion, a refund or cancellation of contract may be sought. ☐

What are the terms and conditions? ☐

Have you read and approved the terms and conditions? ☐

What is the procedure regarding faulty products, time frame for repair, method and time frame for return and dispute resolution? ☐

What is the procedure for a refund? ☐

You are entitled to a refund within 30 days (section 7(2) of the Directive on Distance Selling). The new EU Consumer Rights Directive reduced the time period for a refund to seven days. ☐

You are entitled to return the goods without additional cost (excluding postage) (section 6(b)). This changes under the EU Consumer Rights Directive if return charges are not estimated at time of delivery. ☐

If the item is not available, do you, as consumer, accept an alternative item (section 9(3) of the Directive on Distance Selling)? You have a right to cancel even alternative items (section 9(b)). ☐

What are the security measures in relation to credit card payments and personal details? The new EU Consumer Right Directive restricts credit/debit or payment fees over and above the actual cost to the trader. ☐

'If in doubt, check it out.' When distance buying, use the same precaution you would use when buying goods from a shop. ☐

Data Protection

I keep getting direct mail from companies and I don't know where they got my details from. What can I do?
If you do not want to receive direct marketing, you have a right to notify the sender that you object to receiving such

material. It is against the law under the Data Protection Acts (section 2) for an organisation not to respect your request to cease sending material to you. It is advisable to put your request in writing and keep a copy. If you continue to receive correspondence after you have objected, you can make a complaint to the Data Protection Commissioner. Apart from contacting organisations individually, you may also wish to avail of a service run by the Irish Direct Marketing Association (IDMA). The IDMA is a non-profit organisation which represents the direct marketing industry. Over 60 organisations are members of the IDMA and every member has to adhere to the standards set by the IDMA in their codes of practice. Under the mail preference service, if you supply your contact details to the IDMA they will circulate these details amongst their members. This will result in most of the main direct marketing companies removing your details from their mailing lists. For more information about the mail preference service, visit the IDMA website (www.idma.ie). There is also an obligation on an organisation that has not obtained your details directly from you to inform you of the original source of your details. This will enable you to contact the original organisation and object to it using or distributing your details for marketing purposes.

Some of the information used to market to you is in the public domain, such as the telephone directory or the Electoral Register. In other situations, marketers generally do not obtain your details unless you have either directly given them your contact details or have supplied contact details in the context of entering a competition, a promotion or some form of survey. If you are supplying contact details in these circumstances it is important to read the entry conditions carefully in order to understand how your contact details may be used. If the conditions state that your details may be used for marketing or may be passed on to third parties, you must judge whether you wish to continue providing the information.

Even where you do supply contact details, you can always change your mind at a later date and inform that organisation that you do not want to receive any further marketing material. In general, when you are asked for your contact details you should ask why they are needed. If you are not satisfied with the reasons offered or do not trust the organisation, you must judge whether you want to provide any information.

Be careful when supplying details on a public space such as a website forum. Details may be viewed by people without your knowledge and used without your consent.

My friend put my photo on Facebook; can she do this without my permission? How can I get the photo removed?

This is an interesting question as we have to understand who is the 'data controller' under the data protection legislation. A data controller is a person who, either alone or with others, controls the contents and use of personal data. Data controllers who obtain information must give you the reason they want the details and, if received from a third party, must advise you from whom they received it. This means that the information must have been gained fairly, must be kept safe and must be available to the person if asked for.

A 'data subject' (the individual) is defined as an individual who is the subject of personal data. 'Personal data', i.e. photos or information, is defined as data relating to a living individual who is or can be identified either from the data or from the data in conjunction with other information that is in, or is likely to come into, the possession of the data controller.

It has been contentiously argued that the individual who owns the page on Facebook is the data controller due to the acceptance of the terms and conditions of the social network site, and the fact that the individual has control over the contents.

Under data protection legislation, the law states that any information stored or held, either on computer or hard copy/photographs, in relation to an individual should be factually correct, only available to those who should have it and only used for the stated purpose.

Therefore, quite simply, if a photo has been put on Facebook without your consent the best thing to do is ask the person to remove it. If they do not, Facebook do have a facility where individuals can report a matter or complaint to them and ask them, as agents or facilitators of the site, to remove the picture.

If you think that an individual may be holding some of your personal details, you can ask them to confirm this within 21 days. If they do have personal details about you, they must tell you which details they hold and the reason why. You can ask for this information free of charge.

The Minister for Justice, Equality and Defence recently launched (in March 2012) a consultation process on the European Commission's proposal for a new Regulation on data protection standards within the EU. The proposed Regulation is intended to replace the 1995 Data Protection Directive, which sets standards for the protection of personal data and transfer of such data within the internal market and to countries outside the EU. The Directive was transposed into Irish law in the Data Protection (Amendment) Act 2003. The proposed new Regulation seeks to update the rules contained in the 1995 Directive in order to take account of the extensive technological change and globalisation which have taken place in the seventeen years since the Directive was adopted.

What are my rights in relation to pictures of me in a public place?

Personal data that is processed only for journalistic, artistic or literary purposes is exempt from compliance with any provision of the legislation as long as it is a matter of public interest and the publication is available to the public. It is always advisable, if in doubt, if publishing photographs for private purposes to seek the permission of the person prior to printing or public display.

Misleading Claims and Advertising

I recently purchased an item that stated it was 'non-odour', but when I brought it home there was a strong smell from it for a period of time. Can I complain about it?

The item can be returned under the Sale of Goods and Supply of Services Act 1980, on the grounds that the item was not 'as described' and the remedy of the three Rs (Repair, Replace, Refund) can be implemented.

With reference to misleading claims, consumers are protected under the Consumer Information Act 1978. Misleading claims are described as making a significant difference to the way a product is presented to such an extent that a 'reasonable' person would have been misled by it. Misleading claims can relate to details such as weight, contents and how the product works or performs. All misleading claims should be reported to the National Consumer Agency (www.nca.ie) for investigation and possible determination. The new Consumer Protection Act 2007 incorporates the EU Unfair Commercial Practices Directive (2005/28/EC), which increases the power of the consumer in relation to any false information that deceives or misleads the average consumer in such a way that impairs them from making an informed choice. Goods must carry specific, clear information and must not omit relevant important information that would assist with an informed choice. Marketing and advertising must also prevent an average consumer from being misled. The Act also protects you regarding the provision of services if standards of skill and the principles of good faith are not complied with. The Act also now provides protection for whistleblowers (people who report breaches).

The maximum fine for a first offence is €3,000, and €60,000 for convictions on indictment. Higher fines are also in place for repeat offenders. At present, a Public Consultation on Directive 2006/114/EC concerning misleading and comparative advertising and on unfair commercial practices affecting businesses has commenced (up to December 2011) pending further review.

Does this also relate to the supply of services, e.g. if a shop advertises as offering 24-hour service but is actually closed at any given hour?

Yes, the Consumer Protection Act 2007 also applies to the provision of services. False statements must not be made intentionally.

Statements should only be made when there is a strong reason to believe they are true with specific reference to the delivery, location and service level expected. Under the Sale of Consumer Goods and Associated Guarantees Regulations 2003, such statements may cause a reasonable consumer to be 'misled', and it may be difficult for a seller to prove that the statement did not influence the consumer's decision. The Consumer Protection Act 2007 also protects against misleading advertising.

I was in a shop recently and items were on display with a sign 'reduced from €30 to €20'. I never saw the items on display before. Can they do this?
When an item is on sale, it should have been displayed at the previous 'higher' price for at least 28 successive days in the previous 3 months. Prices displayed must not be false or misleading regarding current or previous prices. Prices should not contain hidden 'extras' that are only visible upon inspection or investigation. Any complaints should be made to the National Consumer Agency.

I bought a holiday package after I saw an advertisement in the paper, but on further inspection I feel I was misled. Can I seek compensation?
This may be described as 'bait advertising' and an unfair and misleading inducement. All adverts in the press, media, signs, posters and direct mail must be legal, decent, honest and truthful. The key question is whether the advert misled you. The burden of proof is on the advertiser to ensure the advert is accurate and factual. Complaints should be made to the National Consumer Agency. The new Consumer Protection Act 2007 puts the burden of proof on the retailer to ensure information is not concealed from the consumer and that such information is not unclear or ambiguous. Advertisers can only be exempt if they 'did not knowingly' believe the advertisement to be misleading.

It may be possible to take out an order preventing publication of a certain advertisement (European Communities Misleading Advertising Regulation 1988).

In a situation where you have been affected financially by such an advertisement you may have a case against the person or organisation for compensation.

Signs and Notices

What does the saying 'your statutory rights are not affected' mean?
Your statutory rights are your specific rights under the Sale of Goods and Supply of Services Act 1980 (as above). Sellers of goods cannot remove their liability by posting any notice refusing to comply with such statutory rights.

A shop I bought an item from has a sign saying 'No Refunds'. Can they do this?
No, a shop cannot refuse you a refund, assuming the item is faulty, is not fit for its intended purpose, does not do what it is meant to do and is not what you thought you were buying from the sample you were shown. This is in breach of section 11(2) of the Sale of Goods and Supply of Services Act 1980, which states that displays, advertisements, labelling or documents cannot be in place to prevent a buyer of goods or services taking action.

Section 11(3) also states that sellers of goods cannot have signs stating general denial of refunds or exchanges, or declaring that only credit notes are given, as this compromises your rights in cases where the goods are in breach of the fundamental requirements above.

A shop has a sign saying 'No Returns after Six Weeks'. Can they do this?
No, this is not legal, as it is impossible to say when a fault may occur in the future. In this situation the retailer is trying to bypass the consumer's statutory rights. However, the seller may simply be stating his/her policy in relation to exchanges (on non-fault basis) where the customer changes his/her mind (non-statutory rights). This may be quite common after the Christmas period for 'change of mind' returns only.

A shop has a sign saying 'All Items must be Returned with Original Tags'. Can they do this?
Again this is not legal, as a consumer cannot control when or if a product may or may not become faulty. Therefore, it would still be possible to return such an item when or if a fault arises. However, the seller may simply be stating their policy in relation to exchanges (on non-fault basis) where the customer changes their mind (non-statutory rights).

What is the meaning of the saying 'invitation to treat'?
'Invitation to treat' is simply an enticement or opportunity to purchase an item. An 'invitation' does not provide you with any specific rights. Rights and protection occur on purchase (Sale of Goods and Supply of Services Act 1980).

Gift Vouchers

I was given a present of a gift voucher. The voucher has a use-by date of six months in the future. What if I can't use it by then? Can I receive a refund?
Regarding gift vouchers, it is very important to be fully aware of the terms and conditions entered into when

purchasing as there is no specific legislation in this area. Sellers and service providers are within their legal rights to set use-by dates for gift vouchers, if they wish to do so. Therefore the following guidelines should be considered:

- Does the gift voucher have an expiry date? Can this date be extended?
- Are there any restrictions as to how the voucher can be redeemed, i.e. are there situations when the gift voucher cannot be used?
- What happens if the amount spent is less than the amount on the voucher? Is the balance refunded in cash or vouchers?
- Can gift vouchers be transferred?
- What if the voucher is lost?

There is also a presumption that if no use-by date is clearly stated on the gift voucher, the voucher is open-ended, and therefore can be used without any time restrictions up to a maximum six-year period (under the Statute of Limitations), although this may be extended at the discretion of the seller.

Therefore, in relation to your query, it is advisable to discuss the issue with the shop or seller to fully clarify the terms and conditions regarding use of vouchers.

The new Consumer Protection (Gift Voucher) Bill 2009 proposes to enforce a five-year validation period for all gift vouchers. Breach of this section by retailers will give consumers the right to seek damages. This is a Private Members' Bill and is not on the Government Legislative Programme for 2012 or the foreseeable future.

I had a gift voucher for a shop. I now believe the shop is closing down. What can I do to get my money back?
If you have gift vouchers for a certain shop, ideally the first thing to do is to contact the shop to see if there are any arrangements in place regarding refunds. Alternatively you could find out from the shop who the appointed liquidator or receiver is and write to them. Unfortunately, customers with gift vouchers would not be ranked high in importance when it comes to debts. The priority when it comes to debts are secured loans, Revenue and employee cost. Customers with gift vouchers will be ranked at the bottom of the list along with creditors (suppliers to whom the shop owes money).

If you are not aware who the appointed liquidator or receiver is, or the shop is now closed, contact the Companies Registration Office (www.cro.ie) as they will advise you accordingly. You will then need to write to the liquidator or receiver providing them with all relevant paperwork (copies of vouchers, dates, times and so on). Subject to money being available during this process, you may receive payment, part payment or, unfortunately, no payment. You can alternatively submit a claim through the Small Claims Court (discussed later), but even if you win your case there may not be any money available to pay your claim.

Legal Tender

My local shop refuses to accept €50 and €100 notes. Is it not legal tender? Can they legally do this?
Yes, they may be able to do this. It is important that the notice is openly displayed in the shop or before reaching the till or counter, to ensure individual consumers

are not intentionally affected or discriminated against. Therefore consumers can make an informed decision before purchasing.

The toll bridge will not accept copper coins (1c, 2c and 5c). Can they do this?

Yes, similar to the previous answer, they may be able to do this, but it is essential such notices be openly displayed in advance of the transaction.

Deposits

I paid a deposit for an item last month. The price has now been reduced. Do I pay the full price?

You reserve an item at the price it is at the time the transaction takes place. It is important to discuss the situation with the seller at the time to confirm how long the item will be reserved for if the balance is not paid within a specified timeframe, the possibility of reducing the price to the sale price, if applicable, and what happens to the deposit if you, the buyer, cancels.

I bought an item and paid a deposit. I now wish to change my mind. Can I get my deposit back?

The refund of a deposit is purely at the discretion of the seller. Depending on the policy of the shop, you may be able to use the deposit to purchase other items or you may forfeit (lose) the deposit. Therefore, it is very important to confirm fully all details with the seller before entering into a transaction.

Does every payment of a deposit have a 'cooling-off' period?

'Cooling-off' periods are generally only applicable in distance selling (shopping online – discussed later), financial services contracts and changing service providers, unless otherwise stated in the terms and conditions of the transaction. Therefore, as a general rule, there is no 'cooling-off' period when paying/reserving an item by deposit and therefore it is essential to be aware of all the contractual details prior to payment as deposits can only be returned at the seller's discretion if you change your mind.

Purchasing by Credit

I bought an item from a shop by credit. Do my rights change regarding any faults?

No, your rights regarding faults are not removed if you purchase items by credit. It is important to distinguish by which credit method you purchased the items, i.e. hire purchase, instalments, etc., in relation to the goods title. The title or ownership doesn't pass to the customer until the final instalment in many hire purchase cases, but this does vary from credit agreement to credit agreement.

The same principles apply to faults that may occur with an item purchased (Sale of Goods and Supply of Services Act 1980) and the remedies are still the three Rs (Repair, Replace, Refund). Under section 14 of the Act, the finance house (company providing credit, if any) is jointly answerable with the seller to the buyer of goods if a breach/ misrepresentation occurred in the sale of the goods. It is therefore important to check who is responsible if there are problems within the agreement, and with whom the responsibility lies in each case.

With reference to hire purchase (HP) agreements, specific provisions are made during the lifetime of the credit arrangement. In such arrangements, the goods are not fully owned by you, the consumer, until the last payment is made. However, if you have paid one-third of the price (agreement price), the item cannot be re-possessed without a court order. In 2011 the High Court ruled that consumers do not need to have paid half of the HP price before the item can be returned to the finance company (as was previously interpreted to 'terminate' the contract – section 63, Consumer Credit Act 1995), but the court ruling stated that once an item is returned to the finance company, it can be sold on but the HP consumer is still liable until the entire debt has been paid. Therefore, it would be advisable to check the following:

- All the small print in the contract.
- The interest rates and total charges, over and above the normal price.
- If there is a 'cooling off' period, i.e. a time to reflect and opt out of the agreement if you wish to do so.
- Your legal rights regarding such agreements. Check out www.itsyourmoney.ie or contact the Financial Regulator at 1890-777777.

If you purchased such items through other credit arrangements, i.e. instalments or a balloon payment, check the small print for additional charges (if applicable) and/or penalties for early payment prior to the agreed dates.

Caveat emptor ('let the buyer beware') should apply in all cases.

If I purchase an item by cheque or credit card and I am unhappy with the product, can I cancel the cheque or credit card payment?

It is important to have good grounds for cancelling payment, i.e. the goods do not comply with the Sale of Goods and Supply of Services Act 1980. It is then advisable to inform the seller of the goods that you are cancelling the transaction due to noncompliance with the Act. Then, and only then, would it be advisable to consider cancelling the transaction. It is very important to liaise with the seller, as generally title (ownership) only passes upon payment, and a breach of payment may be classed as theft, and non-payment may also affect your credit ratings. Cancellation charges may be applied by your bank or credit card company. It may not be possible to cancel if the transaction has been fully processed by your bank or credit card company.

I bought tickets on the internet for a music concert. I believed I was buying valid original tickets. I paid by credit card. I later found out it was a bogus site. Can I get my money back?

According to section 14 of the Sale of Goods and Supply of Services Act 1980, the finance house (credit card company) and seller are jointly and severally liable to the buyer for any breach of the contract of sale and for any misrepresentations made by the seller (bogus site) with respect to the goods. Therefore, your credit card company is liable for the refund due. It is important to contact your credit card company as soon as possible and advise them of the problem and duly seek a refund as time limits may apply.

CHAPTER 2

Consumer Complaints

Formal Complaints

What should be contained in a formal complaint?
First, it is recommended to keep a copy of all correspondence regarding your complaint (this may be necessary for further action). In the letter clearly state the following:

- The reason for your complaint.
- The specific problem with the product or service, i.e. it is not of merchantable quality, is not fit for the purpose required, is not as described or doesn't correspond with the sample.
- What your complaint is under the Sale of Goods and Supply of Services Act 1980.
- Your required outcome – the three Rs (Repair, Replace, Refund).
- A period of time within which your complaint should be resolved, i.e. on average seven to fourteen working days.
- The next steps if the matter is not resolved amicably, i.e. Small Claims Court (discussed later) and/or possible

legal action (depending on the seriousness of the situation, if you wish to do so).

It is recommended that you send the complaint by registered post and request a receipt/acknowledgement of delivery. If you do not receive a reply, or if agreement can not be reached, you may wish to submit a claim to the Small Claims Court.

Sample Letter (Goods)

Manager's Name and Title
Company Name
Company Address

Date

Re: Complaint in relation to *(product name & serial no./ service)*

Your name, address and contact telephone number

Dear Mr/Mrs/Ms *(Name of Person)*

I wish to make a formal complaint in relation to the *(product/service)* I purchased on *(date and day)*, in *(name of store)*. *(State your reason for complaint and what is wrong with the product.)* I have my receipt as proof of purchase (copy enclosed).

Section 17 of the Sale of Goods and Supply of Services Act 1980 (as incorporated by the 1893 Act) states, 'The seller shall be liable to the buyer for the observance of the terms of the guarantee.' Therefore the seller, not the manufacturer, is responsible for the goods.

Under the legislation, goods must also be of merchantable quality (section 14) and fit for the purpose for which they are required (section 10(14)).

Under section 12(1), the Act implies a warranty, either by the seller, or on behalf of the manufacturer, that spare parts and adequate after-sale service will be made available for a defined period, or a reasonable period of time. This period is currently defined, at most, as the period covered under the Statute of Limitations Act 1957, and is two years for motor vehicles and six years for goods. Rights under a guarantee do not limit the rights of the buyer to the guarantee only, and are provided in addition to the buyer's statutory rights under the Act (section 18).

The three remedies for defective goods or services, under the Sale of Goods and Supply of Services Act 1980, are:

- Repair
- Replace
- Refund

Therefore I would advise you, as the seller, to take corrective action to remedy the situation, at your discretion or by agreement. The enclosed letter can be used in evidence if the matter goes to the Small Claims Court.

In compliance with recommended guidelines, I am providing you with ten days working notice to remedy the above situation before processing my claim with the Small Claims Court.

Please contact me at the enclosed address to confirm acknowledgement of receipt, and you may contact me by phone or in writing to suggest an agreed resolution.

Yours sincerely,

_____

Sample Letter (Services)

Manager's Name and Title
Company Name
Company Address

Date

Re: Complaint in relation to *(service provided – when and how much)*

Your name, address and contact telephone number

Dear Mr/Mrs/Ms *(Name of Person)*

I wish to make a formal complaint in relation to the *(service)* I paid for on *(date and day)* in *(name of store)*. *(State your reason for complaint and what is wrong with the service.)* I have my receipt as proof of purchase (copy enclosed).

Under the legislation (section 39 of the Sale of Goods & Supply of Services Act 1980), the supply of service must be in compliance with the following:

- That the supplier has the necessary skill to render the service.
- That he will supply the service with due skill, care and diligence.
- That, where materials are used, they will be sound and reasonably fit for the purpose for which they are required.
- That, where goods are supplied under the contract, they will be of merchantable quality within the meaning of section 14 (3) of the Act of 1893 (inserted by section 10 of the 1980 Act.

Under section 12(1), the 1980 Act implies a warranty by the provider that spare parts and adequate after-sale service will be made for a defined period, or a reasonable period of time. This period is currently defined, at most, as the period covered under the Statute of Limitations Act (section 13(8)(II)) (two years for motor vehicles).

Section 17 of the Sale of Goods and Supply of Services Act 1980 (as incorporated by the 1893 Act) states, 'The seller shall be liable to the buyer for the observance of the terms of the guarantee.' Therefore the seller, not the manufacturer, is responsible for the goods.

Rights under a guarantee do not limit the rights of the buyer to the guarantee only, and are provided in addition to the buyer's statutory rights under the Act (section 18).

The three remedies for defective goods or services, under the Sale of Goods and Supply of Services Act 1980, are:

- Repair
- Replace
- Refund

Therefore I would advise you, as the provider of the service, to take corrective action, at your discretion or by agreement, to remedy the situation. The enclosed letter can be used in evidence if the matter goes to the Small Claims Court.

In compliance with recommended guidelines, I am providing you with ten days working notice to remedy the above situation before processing my claim with the Small Claims Court.

Please contact me at the enclosed address to confirm acknowledgement of receipt, and you may contact me by phone or in writing to suggest an agreed resolution.

Yours sincerely,

Small Claims Court

What if the complaint is still not resolved?

If your complaint is still not resolved, you may wish to take your complaint to the Small Claims Court. The cost of an application is €25. The Small Claims Court deals with cases regarding the supply of goods and services (seller to consumer) in a transaction. The Small Claims Court also covers minor damage to property (excluding personal injury). The new European Small Claims Court has been agreed by the European Council and has effect in Ireland and Europe (excluding Denmark) since 1 January 2009. Since 11 January 2010, businesses can make claims against other businesses (regarding goods and services) through the Small Claims Court. Business claims are not applicable regarding debts, personal injuries or breach of leasing or hire purchase agreements.

Claims can be submitted through the normal procedure in the jurisdiction in which you reside. The Small Claims Court does not cover private transactions (between two individuals). The maximum claim in the Small Claims Court (since 7 February 2006) is €2,000. Claims for larger amounts can be taken to the District Court (maximum €6,348.69), the Circuit Court (maximum €38,092.14) or the High Court (no limit). In such cases (excluding the Small Claims Court), you may require legal representation and costs may be a factor.

A new Alternative Dispute Resolution (ADR) is being proposed by the European Commission (November 2011) to eliminate the need to go to court for consumer complaints. This would include use of existing ADR organisations in each member state and a European-wide consumer disputes mechanism via a new European-wide online platform to solve contractual disputes within 30 days.

What is the procedure for the Small Claims Court and do I need legal representation?
You must complete an application form (available from the District Court Office or www.courts.ie) and forward

it with the €25 fee to the local District Court. Applications may be submitted online (www.courts.ie), excluding business-to-business and European small claims. It is important to ensure the correct company/trading name and official address is recorded on the form. Incorrect applications may hinder your case.

You (the claimant) do not necessarily need legal representation, as the Small Claims Court was initiated to help people represent themselves. If you have legal representation, legal costs are not awarded; therefore you must pay for such representation, regardless of whether you win or lose.

Since 11 January 2010, businesses can make claims against other businesses (regarding goods and services) through the Small Claims Court. Business claims are not applicable with regard to debts, personal injuries, breaches of leasing or hire purchase agreements.

What is the procedure that follows and do I have to appear in court?

Your application, upon receipt by the court, is forwarded to the relevant person or company (respondent). The respondent can accept or reject the complaint.

If the respondent accepts your complaint but does not respond to it within fifteen days, it is uncontested and the court will make an order for the amount due and period of payment.

If the respondent rejects the claim, there is a reason for dispute. An informal meeting may occur to discuss or resolve the dispute. If it cannot be resolved, a court date will be set for the District Court. European small claims are generally dealt with through correspondence. Documents may have to be translated and the costs of this are incurred by you, the applicant. Judgments in one country are recognised across all European jurisdictions.

If a court date is set, you will have to appear in the District Court. It is necessary to bring all relevant documentation and correspondence to support your case. If you require witnesses to attend you are responsible for their costs and travel expenses.

If you win your case, the other side (respondent) is allowed four weeks to pay the amount to the court.

What if the company or person does not pay as agreed?

After the four-week period, if payment is not made, you can contact the Registrar at the District Court and request an order from the court for the Sheriff to seek payment. There is an additional cost for this service, which can be refunded upon successful receipt of the payment due. It is therefore very important to consider taking a case against an organisation, if you truly believe it will be impossible to recoup payment.

SUMMARY CHECKLIST: Formal Complaints

Did you put your complaint in writing? Did you keep a copy? ☐

Did you ensure you sent the letter to the relevant person? ☐

Was it hand delivered, or sent by registered post? ☐

Did you clearly state your complaint, your required outcome, the relevant legislation, time frame for completion, and further possible legal action? ☐

Did you receive a response (formal or otherwise) from the company/service provider? ☐

Did you submit a claim to the Small Claims Court? ☐

Did you include the correct retailer/service provider trading name and address? ☐

Claims submitted with the manufacturer's name and address
are not admissible. ☐

What are you seeking compensation for, and how much do
you seek? (Maximum limit is €2,000 for the Small Claims
Court; damages not rewarded.) ☐

Is your expectation fair and reasonable, and what was the
actual damage caused? ☐

Has the person/business you have taken action against
accepted/rejected liability? ☐

Is the person/business liquid? Do they have money to meet
your claim? ☐

If you decide to have legal representation, be aware that
legal costs are not awarded. ☐

If representing yourself in court, ensure you have a comprehensive record of all the facts. ☐

Where to Complain

Broadcasting (TV/Radio)

*I was listening to a radio programme yesterday. I was
appalled at the inappropriate language used on the programme, especially considering the time of day it was
broadcast. To whom can I complain?*
You may wish to further your complaint with the
Broadcasting Authority of Ireland (BAI). The BAI deals
with complaints in relation to radio and television broad-
casters licensed in Ireland. Complaints can relate to
impartiality of news and current affairs, taste and decency
(violence, sex and inappropriate language), privacy
(unreasonably approaching or pestering people) and slan-
der (inaccurate facts affecting the perception or image of
a person). It would be advisable to make your complaint
within 30 days of the broadcast. Such content may also

include advertisements. For further information contact the BAI at 01-6441200 (www.bai.ie).

Builders

I bought a new house recently and there appears to be a problem with the flooring (it's uneven). The builder won't come back and repair it. What can I do?
First, it is important to confirm whether you are protected under the HomeBond Scheme, i.e. whether your builder is registered with HomeBond. The HomeBond Scheme provides protection for non-structural defects (within one year), structural defects of the house and adherence to building standards. Non-structural defects may include leaky plumbing, lack of insulation and uneven flooring. Structural defects include such issues as subsidence. It is advisable to fully inform your builder (in writing) of your concerns and issues of dispute. If the builder ignores you or does not complete such work to a reasonable standard, you may refer your complaint to HomeBond. HomeBond will try to mediate with the builder or set up an arbitration. In some cases, HomeBond may arrange for such works to be completed by an alternative builder and redirect costs to the original builder. In addition, of course the Sale of Goods and Supply of Services Act 1980 (as discussed earlier) also protects you in relation to the skill, care and diligence (regarding materials and fitting) that should have been taken when carrying out the work. A complaint can be made under this legislation, depending on the cost of repair, to the District Court (maximum €6,348.69), the Circuit Court (maximum €38,092.14) or the High Court (no limit).

If the builder is not registered, you may need to seek legal advice in relation to a possible breach of contract and a possible breach of a duty of care (reasonable foreseeability or negligence) by the builder in relation to standards of workmanship. Alternatively, you may be able to complain about a specified builder if they are registered with the Construction Industry Federation (CIF). For further information, please contact HomeBond at 1850-306300 (www. homebond.ie) or the Construction Industry Federation at 01-4066000 (www.cif.ie). In addition, it is important to check that your builder is a member of the Irish Home Builders Association (IHBA). If so, the buyer is protected under the Home Purchase Protection Pledge (HPPP).

Car Insurance

What should I do if I am in a car accident with another vehicle? Is there any cover if the other car has no insurance?
If the accident is serious, cars should not be moved from the scene of the accident. Car engines should be turned off and the handbrakes applied. If the accident is minor, cars can be moved, taking care to mark the road where the accident occurred as well as warning oncoming traffic. If a person is injured, the Gardaí and/or ambulance service should be contacted. Don't give an injured person anything to eat or drink. Make sure the scene is safe for you and for others. You must remain at the scene for a reasonable period of time. Both parties involved in the accident must provide information to each other (or someone on their behalf). It may be advisable to take photos and detail the circumstances of the accident. In addition, if a Garda is present, he or she may require personal details and motor insurance details. If there is no Garda present, the accident

should be reported to the nearest Garda Station as soon as possible.

If you are in a car accident where the other car is uninsured or cannot be identified (for example, in the case of a 'hit and run'), it is important to log your accident with the Motor Insurers' Bureau of Ireland (MIBI) (www.mibi. ie). You will be required to complete a Claim Notification Form (available online). For personal injuries, medical reports will also be required. In some cases, compensation may be sought for damaged vehicles (against unidentified vehicles) if there is substantial personal injury. Claims should be submitted as soon as possible. The MIBI also deals with claims in relation to foreign registered vehicles. For further information, contact 01-6769944.

I had a car accident recently. In my opinion it was not my fault. I am led to believe my insurance company has already paid out. What can I do?
It is important to discuss these issues with your insurance company and seek clarification on the status of the claim. You may wish to seek further information from the Insurance Information Service at 01-6761914 (www.iif.ie). This service can assist you with information on a variety of situations regarding motor insurance.

If, having written to the insurance company and having sought clarification of your claim or the decision made, you are unhappy with the response given, you may wish to seek an independent review of your complaint. The Financial Ombudsman (assuming your insurance company is included in its members) may re-assess your complaint. The Ombudsman has the power to award compensation and/or enforce the compliance of companies with such outcomes.

Cold Calling

I am tired of receiving phone calls at home from companies requesting me to switch telecom providers or trying to sell me services. Can I prevent them from contacting me?
Yes. 'Cold calling', as it is commonly known, is the method of contacting you by phone to sell you services. If you would prefer for this not to happen, contact your telecoms provider, i.e. the provider to whom you pay your line rental. You must inform them of your request to be removed from the National Directory Database (NDD) (there is no fee for this service). The NDD is a list of all phone numbers contained in public phone books or available through directory enquiries (Republic of Ireland only).

Your request should be processed within five working days, or twenty-eight days at the latest. If you continue to receive calls thereafter, inform the company of your request to be removed from their mailing list, request details of their company name and make a complaint to the Data Protection Commissioner (Canal House, Station Road, Portarlington, Co. Laois; 1890-252231; www.dataprotection.ie).

If you specifically requested such calls (through a request on an application or order form), you should cancel this service by contacting the company directly.

Dentists

I have a complaint about my dentist. He charged me a fee for being late for my appointment. As I am covered under a Medical Card (for dental care), to whom should I complain?
Since 1 January 2007, a new procedure for complaints is in place in relation to the HSE. Such complaints cover

services provided directly by the HSE or indirectly by third parties acting for the HSE. Therefore, in such a situation, the HSE is the body to which you complain. Valid grounds for complaints may include unfair administrative procedures, including carelessness or impartial decisions. A complaint may not be applicable if the matter is covered in legal proceedings or clinical decisions (medical decisions).

Since 1 June 2011 all dental practices must display private fees (including a minimum and maximum price) in an area visible to patients before their consultation. This became mandatory under the Code of Practice by the Dental Council. In addition, under the EU/IMF deal, measures will be taken to remove restrictive practices across a number of legal professions.

Written complaints will be acknowledged within five working days, and investigated within thirty working days. If you are still unhappy with the outcome, you have a right to complain to the Ombudsman. Complaints about dentists can be made to the Dental Council (established under the Dentist Act 1985). Dentists must comply with the code of practice covering areas such as professional behaviour and dental ethics. Complaints can be made to the Dental Council, 57 Merrion Square, Dublin 2, or call 01-6762069 (www.dentalcouncil.ie).

Doctors

My doctor has prescribed me medication, but did not warn me of possible side effects. To whom can I complain?
If you feel you are unhappy with your GP, you may wish to complain to the Medical Council at 01-4983100 (www. medicalcouncil.ie). In addition, if you have any complaints

in relation to health matters, information can be found on www.healthcomplaints.ie. This site provides information in relation to hospitals, GPs, nursing homes, child services and mental health and disability services. It is advisable to put your complaint in writing clearly stating your concern and the full details of your case. The issue of possible medical negligence and a breach of a duty of care may have to be considered. The Medical Council will need to assess the seriousness of your complaint and take appropriate action (disciplinary action if required). The Medical Practitioners Act 2007 states that the Medical Council's main role is the protection of public interest. The Act sets down the establishment and monitoring of professional standards as well as registration of doctors and investigation of complaints.

The Medical Practitioners Amendment Act 2011 now regulates doctors so that they must be registered in order to practise medicine in Ireland. Providing false information regarding insurance will impose a summary fine of €5,000 and/or six months in prison. On conviction, the fine will be from €130,000 to €320,000 and one to five years' imprisonment will apply. The Medical Practitioners Act 2007 (Amendment) (Medical Indemnity) Bill proposes to make it mandatory for registration purposes for all medical practitioners engaged in clinical practice to have in place adequate clinical indemnity cover. The Medical Practitioners Act 2007 (Amendment) (No. 2) Bill also proposes to amend the Medical Practitioners Act 2007 in relation to a number of issues.

Driving Instructors

I have a complaint about my driving instructor. Should he be registered? Where can I complain?
Since 1 January 2009 all driving instructors should be registered with the Road Safety Authority (www. rsa.ie). Instructors must display an approved driving instructor (ADI) permit. For further information check www.drivingtest.ie.

Electricity Providers

I have a complaint about my electricity provider. I was sold a product and now want to 'switch' back. Also I am having difficulty paying my bill. What can I do? Who can I complain to?
If you are unhappy with the method or aggressive selling of energy provision, you should first make a formal complaint to the energy provider. Every energy provider must have a customer charter clearly covering all areas, including billing, bill pay and arrears, marketing, complaints and disconnections. If you are still unhappy, you can progress your complaint to the Commission for Energy Regulation (CER). As with all complaints, a detailed report (and copy of correspondence) should be provided as well as any reference numbers (if applicable). A complaint form from the CER is available from www.energycustomers.ie. On average, complaints can take approximately three months to resolve.

Since June 2011 a new Code was established by the Commissioner for Energy Regulation which will allow energy providers to 'flag'customer arrears before allowing them to switch provider (known as 'debt hopping').

Customers who are 56 days in arrears, with bills of €200 or more, will be 'flagged' for the new provider before the switch takes place. All providers must have this system in place by 1 January 2013 and ensure it is in compliance with data protection legislation.

In addition, since November 2011, the Commission for Energy Regulation (CER) has requested that all energy providers be more empathetic when it comes to structured payment plan options for customers in debt and/or the provision of 'Pay As You Go' electricity or gas meters. In relation to disconnections, every energy supplier must have a code of practice clearly setting out its process and procedure in dealing with debt, specifying clearly notice periods for disconnections and payment plans and recognising debt management groups or organisations, i.e. Money Advice and Budgeting Service (MABS). In addition, all Codes of Practice must be pre-approved by the CER in advance. The CER have reiterated that 'vulnerable' customers (definition set out in European legislation) should not be disconnected during the winter period. People with medical conditions who depend on electrically powered equipment, such as home dialysis machines, oxygen concentrators or artificial ventilators, should complete a priority register form. This form, available from all suppliers, ensures you are contacted in advance of any scheduled or unscheduled outages as soon as they are discovered.

The cost of disconnection and reconnection is set at €70 and €61.74 (ex. VAT) respectively for electricity and gas.

Financial Services

I recently had a dispute with my bank regarding charges. The bank did not take my complaint seriously. What can I do?

First, it is always advisable to forward a complaint in writing to your bank, clearly stating the reason for your complaint and recommended outcomes for resolution.

You may wish to seek financial information from the Financial Regulator (1890-777777) to clarify your situation. The Regulator's role is to assist consumers with their protection in the financial sector.

A new co-operation agreement between the offices of the Financial Regulator, Financial Services Ombudsman and Pensions Ombudsman came into effect on 1 April 2006 to assist consumers in their dealings with financial services firms. Also, since 1 June 2006, the new Market Abuse (Directive 2003/6/EC) Regulation 2005 came into operation. This will now prevent unsolicited automatic loan approvals arriving by post, and will prevent automatic increases in credit card limits without your consent.

If, upon such assistance, no resolution has been recommended by your bank, you may wish to seek the intervention of the Financial Ombudsman. The Financial Ombudsman is a statutory officer who deals independently with complaints from consumers about their individual dealings with all financial service providers that have not been resolved by the providers. The Financial Ombudsman became a statutory body on 1 April 2005 (www.financialombudsman.ie) and incorporated the voluntary Ombudsman for Credit Institutions and Insurance Ombudsman. Any decisions after investigation by the Ombudsman are binding (enforceable) on the credit institution.

Food Safety

What do I do if I purchased food in an establishment that made me ill? How do I complain about a dirty establishment?

First, contact your local Environmental Health Officer at your nearest HSE centre. It would be advisable to keep any remaining part of the item consumed for investigation. It is also important to keep a record of the date, time and location of consumption, and retain all wrapping or packaging to assist in the investigation. The Food Safety Authority of Ireland (FSAI), as the statutory body, can also assist further with your queries or questions through their advice line at 1890-336677 (www.fsai.ie). The FSAI is responsible for ensuring all food produced and distributed meets the highest standards of safety and hygiene, and complies with the codes of good practice.

Also, the new EU Food Hygiene package came into force on 1 January 2006. The package covers rules on the hygiene of foodstuffs, and specific hygiene and control rules for food of animal origin. General rules are laid down for all food, while specific measures are included for meat and eggs (including products), fishery products, milk and dairy products, frogs' legs, snails and animal fats. The basic rule is that responsibility for safe food rests with the food operators who are involved in the production, manufacture, processing, distribution or retail of the food. All food operators have to be registered and they are obliged to apply compulsory self- checking programmes and follow the Hazard Analysis and Critical Control Point (HACCP) principles in all sectors of the food industry (except farms). Primary producers (farmers) must protect, as far as possible, primary products against contamination.

New regulations also state rules on the production, transport, storage and handling of animal feed. As with food operators, feed businesses have primary responsibility for ensuring the safety of products put on the market. They will have to apply the HACCP self-checking principles, keep records of production and marketing, be registered with the national authorities and undergo man-datory training. They will be obliged to pay for the costs, such as withdrawal from the market and destruction of feed, if something goes wrong. EU Member States will be required to draw up annual control and contingency plans which the Food and Veterinary Office (FVO) of the EU will evaluate.

Gardaí

I wish to make a complaint regarding my local Gardaí on grounds of harassment. What can I do?
Complaints regarding Gardaí can be made to the Garda Ombudsman (an independent statutory body, functioning since 8 May 2007). Under section 83 of the Garda Síochána Act 2005, a complaint can be made by any member of the public who was directly affected or who witnessed misbehaviour by a Garda. Complaints can be made by anyone aged seventeen and over and by guardians of individuals aged under seventeen. A complaint may be made to any member of the Gardaí, at any Garda Station, or directly to the Garda Ombudsman by phone, fax or via the website (1890-600800; www.gardaombudsman.ie).

Complaints may be made in relation to the death of, or serious harm to, a person in custody (section 91), or relate to the conduct of a Garda including discourtesy, neglect of duty, abuse of power, corruption and/or being drunk (both on and off-duty). The Garda Ombudsman can also enter premises, search, arrest, detain, charge or summon a person, and take samples, fingerprints and photographs. The powers are also extended to include searching Garda stations and taking possession of evidence.

Complaints must be made within six months of the incident (section 84), although such time may be extended if there are good reasons for doing so. Section 110 may impose fines and/or imprisonment if misleading information is given in relation to a complaint. Complaints may be resolved either informally, by mediation, or by formal investigation. Outcomes may include disciplinary proceedings (against the Gardaí) or prosecution by the Director of Public Prosecutions.

Can I access information held on me by the Gardaí?
Section 4 of the Data Protection Act 1988 (and 2003, as amended) allows you to make a request for any personal data being kept by the Gardaí about you. You are entitled to know what information is stored about you, for what purpose, where the information was received, and any person to whom the Gardaí disclosed the information. Requests must be replied to (even if unsuccessful) within 40 days.

Information may be refused if it identifies other parties, i.e. possible sources, or if information is being held for the purpose of preventing or investigating a crime.

The Gardaí may even access information about you from other sources (and the third parties must oblige) if the data is required for the purpose of safeguarding security or preventing a possible crime.

To apply for your information, you must send €6.35 to the Garda Central Vetting Unit, Racecourse Road, Thurles,

Co. Tipperary. You must include your date of birth, previous address (in the Republic), a certified copy of a passport, driving licence or birth certificate, and your fee.

Health Insurance

The price of Health Insurance is on the increase again. Can I switch provider without penalty and what happens if I have a dispute? What are my rights under the normal public health system if I cancel my provide health insurance?

The Health Insurance Authority is the statutory regulator in the area of private health insurance in Ireland (www. hia.ie). It is always essential to shop around in relation to insurance policies to ensure you get the best value for money and the best plan in comparison to competitors. The Health Insurance Authority also provides a website (www.healthinsurancecomparison.ie) to allow you compare policies (or your existing policy) in relation to what services you require and which policy is best value for you.

You have a right to change your health insurance plan or insurer without penalty (unless you wish to upgrade your policy and the waiting periods only relate to the additional services requested as part of this upgrade. This may vary from provider to provider, depending in each circumstance). If you wish to cancel mid policy there may be termination clauses so it is very important to check the small print of your policy.

If you have a complaint in relation to your insurance provider it is important to put your complaint in writing and to try to resolve the matter with your provider in the first instance. If you are still unhappy, you can either contact the Health Insurance Authority or make a complaint to the Financial Services Ombudsman. The decision of the Ombudsman is binding and can only be appealed to the High Court.

If you cancel your private health insurance and re-apply within thirteen weeks, you may still be covered; however, if the period of lapse is greater than thirteen weeks, you have to recommence your 'waiting' cover period. If your policy has lapsed or has been cancelled completely, the public health service provides you with the following basic service:

- Everyone in Ireland, regardless of nationality, can avail of public hospital services (subject to 'ordinary' residence conditions set by the HSE, i.e. proof of residence here). If you are not ordinarily resident, you will have to pay the full economic costs of medical attention.
- Accident and emergency cover (€100 charge or no fee if referred by your GP). You are entitled to free outpatient (follow-up) visits if they are related to the initial visit. In cases of excessive hardship, the HSE may waive the fee.
- Free outpatient visits (x-rays, tests, etc.) and procedures (no overnight stay), if referred by your GP, and free consultant visits. A list of waiting times for procedures is available on the Patient Treatment Register website (www.ptr.ie). You are not entitled to choose the consultant who will see you.
- Free maternity services for women and free accident and emergency for children up to six weeks of age. Free accident and emergency is also available to children (referred by a GP or with certain disabilities).
- In-patient hospital stay or care at a fee of €75 per day for a maximum of ten days (€750) in any twelve-month consecutive period.

- Free treatment for people with prescribed infectious diseases.
- Free hospital services for people under EU Regulations (i.e. persons in receipt of a European Health Insurance Card. This service is also available to Irish people travelling abroad on holidays – www.ehic.ie).
- Free mental health service for children under the age of sixteen.
- Free vaccination and immunisation for children.
- Free hospital cover for children up to age sixteen (if the defect is found during the school examination), free health examination at health centres/clinics provided by the HSE for children up to the age of six attending national school, and free dental services provided by the HSE up to the age of fifteen.
- Free medication and appliances to people in receipt of the Long-Term Illness Card.
- Maximum prescription costs per month per family of €132 under the Drug Payment Scheme (DPS).

In addition, you can apply for a Medical Card (free GP visits, public hospitals stays and free medication, subject to 50c fee per dispensed item and a maximum monthly fee of €10 (for 20 items)) or a GP Card (free GP visits only), which are means tested. Under the tax system you can seek a rebate of all medical costs and procedures (public stays, medication costs, specialist fees and any excess costs paid under your private medical insurance cover) at a rate of 20 per cent (no initial entry threshold or upper cap) using the MED 1 form.

Licensed Premises

I went to a pub recently and the price charged for a drink was different to the price displayed. What can I do?
The Retail Price (Beverages in Licensed Premises) Display Order 1999 requires that prices be displayed outside and inside premises and indicate where prices may vary (e.g. in the lounge or late at night). For future reference, ensure to pay only the displayed price or contact the manager. Complaints should be made to the National Consumer Agency for investigation.

I was recently refused entry to a nightclub. I was told by the bouncer 'regulars only', even though people before and after me were not 'regulars'. Who can I complain to?
Equality legislation is in place under the Equal Status Acts 2000–2004 (as amended) to prevent discrimination regarding the provision of goods and services under the following nine grounds:

- Age
- Race
- Religion
- Gender
- Member of the travelling community
- Marital status
- Disability
- Family status
- Sexual orientation

Discrimination in relation to refusal of entry to a licensed premises is now not covered under the Equality Act 2000 (2004, as amended), or directly under the remit of the

Equality Authority, but under the Intoxicating Liquor Act 2003. Therefore, in such situations, it is advisable to write to the owner of the licensed premises asking the specific reason why you were refused entry (it would advisable to provide as much supporting information as possible, e.g. date, time, venue, etc.) and make your complaint as soon as is practical. If you do not receive a reply, or you are unhappy with the response, you may seek to make a complaint to your local District Court. Under section 19(2) of the Intoxicating Liquor Act 2003, a person who claims that prohibited conduct has been directed against him or her at the point of entry to a licensed premises may apply to the District Court for redress. Under section 19(3), the court may, upon assessment of the complaint, order that compensation be paid to the person (up to the maximum amount allowable in the District Court – €6,348.69), and ensure that the licensed premises complies with the order of the court or order a temporary closure. The Equality Authority may (in their own right) make a complaint against a licensed premises if there are valid and important matters of principle (Intoxicating Liquor Act 2003, section 19(7)). Action taken by an individual may be used in evidence when the hearing for the renewal of the licence is considered by the courts (Intoxicating Liquor Act 2003, section 19(10)).

I see people being served in pubs when they have already had too much to drink. Should the pub stop serving someone if they are drunk?
Yes, under section 4 of the Intoxicating Liquor Act 2003, a licensee shall not supply drink to a drunken person, or any person on a licensed premises buying drink for a drunken person. The licensee should not even admit a person to a

bar who is drunk. Offences of such nature can bring a fine of €1,500 for a first offence, unless the licensee can show they took reasonable steps to prevent the drunkenness taking place. Even a drunk person leaving a pub is presumed to have been drunk whilst on the premises. Section 25 of the Act allows a licensee to prevent the sale of alcohol to people over eighteen years of age if signage is in place stating such a policy on the outside of the premises, and it is carried out in good faith. If valid and carried out correctly, complaints regarding discrimination on grounds of age would not be eligible.

Fines can be imposed on a person buying drink for a drunken person. A drunken person must leave the premises upon request by the licensee or the Gardaí. Breach of such order can impose a fine. Persons acting disorderly in licensed premises may also be fined and/or arrested (sections 5-8).

Motor Industry

I recently left my car in to be repaired. I was told they had fixed the problem. The same problem has reoccurred two weeks later. The garage says it's not their problem. What can I do?

First, it is important to ensure you received a full report of the repair work completed at the time of repair. If you have noticed the same problem recurring, you should contact the garage, discuss the situation and seek clarification. Under the Sale of Goods and Supply of Services Act 1980 the period of time protected in relation to the sale of motor vehicles is two years (section 13(8)(I)(d)) (buyer to consumer, excluding private transactions). The same principle applies under the above Act in relation to goods being of merchantable quality, fit for the purpose required, as described, or as per sample, for both new and used cars. The Act states (section 13(2)) that, at the time of delivery, the vehicle must be free of any defect that would render it a danger to the public, including the driver or passengers. If no progress is made regarding reviewing the re-occurrence of the fault, it would be advisable to put your complaint in writing to the garage, clearly specifying your complaint and setting down a reasonable remedy and time frame for repair.

If the time frame has elapsed without resolution, it is important to ensure the garage is a registered member of the Society of the Irish Motor Industry (SIMI). If the garage is registered, follow up your complaint to the SIMI for investigation. SIMI's remit is in relation to complaints regarding both new and second-hand vehicles. SIMI will try to resolve or remedy the dispute, or the matter may be referred to the Motor Industry Tribunal. Complaints to SIMI must be made in writing within three months.

If no resolution can be found, legal action may be taken, i.e. to the Small Claims Court (if the value is less than €2,000) or, depending on the value of the work or vehicle, to a higher court (District or Circuit). It may be advisable to seek legal opinion in such cases.

SUMMARY CHECKLIST: Complaints to the Motor Industry

Always check the garage is a registered SIMI member.	☐
Be aware the period of time under protection is two years (under the Sale of Goods and Supply of Services Act 1980, section 18(8)(I)(d)).	☐
Clearly specify the problem and request a quotation and time frame for completion.	☐

If in doubt, don't be afraid to seek a second opinion from an
alternative garage. ☐

Ensure you receive a detailed report of all work completed and
a receipt for payment. ☐

Request (where possible) a warranty or guarantee from the
garage for such work (in addition to your statutory rights). ☐

Report any issues to the SIMI for investigation (if registered). ☐

Keep a copy of all correspondence for future reference. ☐

Seek legal opinion, if further action for redress is to be taken
(dependent on the monetary value sought). ☐

Nursing Homes

*I am not happy with the level of service in the nursing
home in which my mother resides. Who can I complain to
and what can be done?*

In May 2007, the Health Information and Quality
Authority (HIQA) was established on a statutory basis
(via the Health (Miscellaneous Provisions) Act 2007). This
Act supports changes in the registration and inspection
of residential institutions (including nursing homes), and
accommodates the investigation of standards of service in
the interests of the health, safety and welfare of persons
in attendance. This remit would also cover private nursing care if financial or other support is provided by the
HSE. Under the Act, 'whistleblowers' are protected in the
health service. The protection applies when the disclosure
is made in good faith. In addition, residential homes for
people with disabilities will also now be inspected by the
HIQA in compliance with existing standards.

If registration of a centre is cancelled, the HSE is responsible for making alternative arrangements for the residents,

or for taking control of a designated centre (with the consent of the provider or by order of the District Court). A centre must give the HSE six months' notice of their intention to close.

Therefore your complaint can be made to the HSE under the complaints procedure introduced on 1 January 2007. A new Health Information Bill plans to provide a legislative framework for the governance of information in the health sector as well as to enhance individual patient care and safety.

Pensions

I recently turned 65. I had a private pension (Personal Retirement Savings Account (PRSA)), and now with the economic crisis I have lost half of my investment. Should my pension provider not have moved my investment to a safer fund well in advance of my retirement? What can I do?

First, it is advisable to make your complaint in writing to your pension provider. The company should have an internal policy and procedure for the investigation of complaints and/or an Internal Dispute Resolution (IDR) procedure. If you are unhappy with the response, you can make a complaint to the Pensions Ombudsman. The remit of the Pensions Ombudsman is only in the areas of occupational or PRSA pensions. The Ombudsman does not cover social welfare pensions, personal pensions (i.e. insurance contracts, which would be covered by the financial ombudsman) or Approved Retirement Funds/Approved Minimum Retirement Funds (ARFs/AMRFs). The remit of the Ombudsman includes maladministration, e.g. neglect, delay, incompetence, incorrectly sold pensions, etc., and/

or actual financial loss. Complaints can be made for periods relating to the last six years (maximum), although this may be extended by the Ombudsman. Complaints should be made in writing to the Ombudsman's Officer (with all supporting documentation). For further information, see www.pensionsombudsman.ie.

Pharmacists

I left a prescription into my chemist recently. Upon collection, I noticed the dosage was double what was intended. If I had not noticed it, there could have been serious medical concerns. To whom can I complain?
If you feel there was a clear breach of a duty of care and possible medical negligence by the pharmacist, you may feel obliged to make such a complaint in writing (including all relevant details) to the pharmacy directly or to the Pharmaceutical Society of Ireland (PSI). Since 1 January 2009, all pharmacies must be registered with the PSI. The role of the PSI is to regulate the practice of pharmacy. For further details, contact 01-2184000 (www.pharmaceuticalsociety.ie). The Pharmacy (No. 1) Act 2007 provides for fitness to practice for pharmacists and the removal of restrictions on pharmacists educated in other EU and EEA countries in relation to establishing in Ireland. Since 1 April 2009, all pharmacies must display a certificate of registration. In addition, each pharmacy must now name a superintendent and supervising pharmacists with at least three years' post-registration experience. A new code of conduct has been introduced since 2009 to improve transparency and patient care. This new code covers six key principles, including patient well-being, safety and care, ensuring professional standards, respecting a patient's

rights and confidentiality, protecting the image of pharmacists, ensuring competency efficiency and effectiveness, and ensuring compliance with the code.

It is proposed under the Health (Amendment) Bill to provide publicly funded GP care without fees at the point of use to claimants of free drugs under the Long-Term Illness Scheme. In addition, the Health (Pricing and Supply of Medicines) Bill proposes to empower the Minister to introduce a system of reference pricing and generic substitution for drugs prescribed under the general medical services and community drug schemes.

Private Health Insurance

I have complained to my private health insurer about my policy. If I want to switch private health insurer, do I have to start my cover from the start? Is there a regulatory body in charge of this area?
It would be advisable to make your complaint directly to your private health insurer first. If you receive an unsatisfactory response, you may wish to make a complaint to the Financial Ombudsman. Alternatively, you can make a complaint to the Health Insurance Authority (www. hia.ie). The Health Insurance Authority (established in February 2001) is the independent regulator in the private health insurance area.

Existing policyholders switching private healthcare providers should be accommodated in relation to time periods spent with their existing policies, and therefore continuation of cover should be accommodated when switching.

Press

I have a complaint about a newspaper. They took a photo of me, and put my name and address in the paper without my permission. What can I do?
The new Office of the Press Ombudsman has been recently established to investigate complaints within the press industry. The Ombudsman proposes to provide a quick, fair and free method of resolving complaints. If the article has directly affected you, and if the code of practice for the industry has been breached, you may have a valid case. You can also make a complaint about the behaviour of a journalist. Newspapers covered include all daily and Sunday newspapers, Irish editions of UK newspapers and regional/provincial newspapers. Complaints must be made within three months of the date of publication. It is advisable to write directly to the editor of the newspaper. If this is unsuccessful, you may then make a complaint to the Ombudsman, including the letter and any response (if received), and a copy of the article in question for investigation. For further details, contact the Office of the Press Ombudsman, 1–3 Westmoreland Street, Dublin 2, or call 1890-208080 (www.pressombudsman.ie).

Solicitors

I am unhappy with both the charges and the services of my solicitor. What can I do?
The role and actions of solicitors are controlled under the Solicitors Acts 1954–2002. First, it may be advisable to make your complaint in writing to your solicitor, setting out your reasons for complaint and proposing a period of time to rectify or remedy the problem. Second, you may

wish to make a complaint to the Law Society of Ireland. It is advisable to disclose fully the nature of your complaint and relevant details in relation to the complaint. Such complaints must be less than five years old. Grounds for complaint may be in relation to:

- Misconduct.
- Inadequate professional service (unprofessional service).
- Excessive fees (such fees may be waived or refunded). You may wish for your bill to be 'taxed' (assessed) by the court official. If your bill is 'taxed', a complaint for overcharging cannot be processed. (The term 'taxing' is a legal term. 'Taxing' in this sense is an independent and impartial assessment of legal costs by an individual in a case, independent of your solicitor's charging system. If you select the 'taxing' method, a date will be set for a hearing. You have an option to seek legal representation for the 'taxing' hearing.)

The Law Society, upon assessment of your complaint, may mediate with your solicitor for resolution or, in serious cases, may follow a more formal investigation (internal committee or disciplinary tribunal).

If you are still unhappy regarding the outcome, you can refer your complaint to the Independent Adjudicator, forwarding all relevant reference details. Complaints to the Adjudicator must not be made any later than three years after the date of the Law Society's final decision.

Initial complaints should be made to the Law Society, Complaints Section, Blackhall Place, Dublin 7 (www.lawsociety.ie). The Civil Law (Miscellaneous Provisions) Act 2008 implemented changes so that the Law Society may direct a solicitor to pay a client up to €3,000 as compensation for loss suffered because of inadequate service. The Act also extends the remit of powers of investigation. The Legal Services Ombudsman Act 2009 outlines the establishment of a Legal Services Ombudsman, whose role will be to investigate complaints after initial complaints to the Law Society. This role will replace the Independent Adjudicator service. The Legal Services Regulation Bill will provide for the regulation of the provision of legal services, to provide for the establishment of the Legal Services Regulatory Authority and to provide for the establishment of the Legal Practitioners Disciplinary Tribunal to make determinations as to misconduct by legal practitioners. The Bill will also provide for new structures in which legal practitioners may provide services together or with others. The Bill will also provide for the establishment of a roll of practising barristers and will reform the law relating to the charging of costs by legal practitioners and the system of assessment of costs relating to the provision of legal services. In addition, the Bill will provide for the manner of appointment of persons to be Senior Counsel and other related matters. The Judicial Council Bill proposes to provide remedies for complaints about judicial misbehaviour, including lay participation in the investigation of complaints.

Taxi Regulator

I want to make a complaint about a taxi driver I had recently. He was extremely rude and unhelpful. What can I do?
The Commission for Taxi Regulation, established on 1 September 2004, is the statutory regulatory body for taxis. Under Regulations 35, 52 and 54 of SI 191 of 1963, as a

consumer you have a right to be treated courteously and helpfully by a driver who is neatly dressed, and to be carried in a vehicle that is clean and roadworthy. If you are unhappy with the driver, it is advisable to ensure you get a printed receipt, as well as the driver and plate details. There is a legal requirement since September 2006 for all taxi drivers to provide a receipt. Under the Finance Bill 2010, the Commission for Taxi Regulation must supply certain information to Revenue as required. Under section 51 of the 2003 Taxi Regulation Act you can complain in relation to the conduct and behaviour of a driver. Complaints should be made in writing, by contacting 1890-606090 or by downloading a complaint form from www.taxiregulator.ie. Responsibility for lost property is still under the remit of An Garda Síochána.

Telecom Providers

I am unhappy with the provider of my telephone services. Whenever I complain I feel they do not take my complaint seriously. What can I do?
Most of the telecoms providers (which include telephone and cable TV) are regulated by Commission for Communication Regulation (ComReg). The role of the regulator is to protect the consumer's interest in the area of service provision. Unfortunately, since September 2003, the Regulator has no direct role in relation to complaints/regulation concerning cable television (i.e. it's unregulated). It is advisable to ensure you have made a formal complaint to your provider (preferably in writing), clearly stating your concerns or complaints, and requesting an investigation or response within a reasonable period of time. Your complaint should be acknowledged by the

provider and a reasonable time frame should be set for investigation or resolution. Most organisations have a customer charter or are guided by codes of conduct set down by the industry. If, after your complaint has been investigated, the outcome is not to your satisfaction, you may make a complaint to the regulating body (ComReg). This complaint should be made within nine months of the original complaint. In serious and extreme cases the licence for the provision of such services by the operator may be restricted or removed.

Under EU reforms (to be transposed into Irish law), the following changes will be implemented:

- The right of European consumers to change, within one day, their mobile and fixed line operator ('porting') whilst keeping their number. In addition, the right to compensation for delays or abuse of the 'porting' procedure.
- Maximum contract periods of twenty-four months (preferably contract periods of no greater than twelve months).
- Better consumer information ensuring consumers are fully aware of what services they are subscribing to, along with itemised billing, service level agreements, and compensation and refunds if the above services are not met.
- Increased protection of data and increased competitiveness without interference.

Complaints regarding premium rate telephone services are regulated by the Regulator of Premium Rate Telecommunications Services (RegTel) (www.regtel.ie; 1850-741741). ComReg (www.comreg.ie) are also the regulatory body for complaints regarding postal services.

Complaints in these cases (regarding An Post) should be made within one month of receiving an item, three months of posting mail in Ireland and within six months of posting international items. Complaints regarding other service providers must be in compliance with their codes of conduct.

For further enquiries, please see www.comreg.ie or contact 1890-229668. Alternatively, you may wish to pursue a complaint under the Sale of Goods and Supply of Services Act 1980 in relation to the required skill, due diligence and care, as well as merchantable quality of the service (it would be advisable to check fully the terms and conditions of your service provider first). You may seek remedy through the Small Claims Court mechanism (if applicable). The Communication Regulation (Premium Rate Services and Electronic Communications Infrastructure) Act 2010 gives ComReg the function to regulate the content and promotion of premium rate services (PRS) as well as to incorporate the transferring of staff from RegTel to ComReg.

CHAPTER 3

Property Rights

Affordable Housing

I want to buy a home but have difficulty in raising a mortgage; what options do I have in relation to affordable housing?
In Budget 2009, the Government announced a new Home Choice Loan for first-time buyers of new and second-hand properties, no larger than 175 metres square (covered by HomeBond Insurance), subject to a maximum value of €285,000 (as 92 per cent of the value) for a maximum loan period of 30 years. This scheme will allow people to access credit where they would not previously have had access. This scheme is operationable since 1 January 2009. The scheme is not available for the purchase of affordable housing. The rate of the loan is 3.95 per cent variable (4.02 per cent APR). The new scheme will be administered by four local authorities (Cork, Dublin, Galway and Kilkenny City Councils) for the whole country. To qualify you must be a first-time buyer and earn more than €35,000 as a single applicant or more than €45,000 between you as joint

applicants. A Home Choice Loan can be refinanced by switching to another financial provider. For more information, contact 1890-252842 or access www.homechoiceloan. ie.

Alternatively, homes are available under the Affordable Housing Scheme administered by local authorities, whereby people can purchase homes at a competitive rate below the normal market rates. It is proposed (since June 2011) that the Affordable Housing Scheme will be discontinued shortly although stocks of homes under this scheme are still available. The scheme is open to EU and EEA citizens who reside and work permanently in Ireland. Under this scheme you could avail of a mortgage from your local authority subject to maximum mortgage amounts and an income means test. Alternatively, mortgages are available from certain financial providers subject to confirmation of eligibility. The mortgage loan can be up to 30 years (from a local authority) or up to 35 years (from a financial provider). In addition you must be a first-time buyer (or separated or divorced). The maximum mortgage is either €220,000 (if provided by a local authority) or 97 per cent of the loan and an assurance that the repayments are no greater than 35 per cent of net income, dependent on your financial provider. The income threshold (which can vary from local authority to local authority) varies from €25,000 to €58,000 for a single applicant to €75,000 for joint applicants. Stamp duty is chargeable on all homes purchased under this scheme since 1 April 2011 at a rate of €100. You must reside in the home and you cannot rent it out (under a landlord–tenant agreement) although you may rent a room under the 'Rent a Room' Scheme where you can earn €10,000 per year tax free (must be declared to Revenue even if under the threshold limit). Total income under this scheme is fully taxable at 20 per cent if the total income exceeds €10,000.

A Mortgage Subsidy Scheme is also in place for people whose earnings are below €28,000 and who have a mortgage from their local authority. The scheme provides a subsidy of between €1,050 and €2,550 per year and is paid directly to the local authority. Alternatively, a Mortgage Allowance Scheme is an allowance of €11,450 payable over five years to tenants (whose income is also below €28,000 and who have a mortgage of at least €38,092.14) purchasing a local authority home. The allowance is paid to the lending body (local authority or finance provider) on a scaled basis.

As you availed of a home at an 'affordable' rate, if you sell the home at any stage up to year 20 you will have to pay a 'clawback'. The 'clawback' rate is the full rate between the purchase price and the market price (at the time of selling) if sold within the first ten years. In cases between year 10 and year 20, the rate is 10 per cent of the difference for every year prior to reaching year 20. There is no 'clawback' rate if selling after year 20. For further information contact your local authority or the Housing and Sustainable Communities Agency (www.housing.ie).

I am renting from the local authority; can I buy out my home or apartment?

If you renting from your local authority and wish to purchase the property (including flats and apartments since 1 January 2012) , the local authority has the discretion to decide if a property in certain areas can be sold or not, subject to certain conditions.

For apartments (under the Tenant Purchase of Apartment Schemes (TPAS) as implemented under the

Housing (Miscellaneous Provisions) Act 2009) since 1 January 2012, there are certain procedures that must be followed. In essence, 65 per cent of all tenants of the apartment complex must support the idea of designating the apartment complex to a 'rent to buy' scheme. Essentially, if approved, the apartment complex will need to be transferred to the ownership of a management company that will manage the relationship and existing payments of rents to the local authority and then ensure the 'rent to buy' tenants have the right to buy. Of course the purchase price will take into account the tenants' income and the number of years a tenant has been renting. Tenants who purchase an apartment will have to be advised of the new rate of service charges to be paid by 'rent to buy' tenant-owners. In addition, the transfer of the designated apartment site will need to be carried out in full consultation with all relevant parties and transparently, and the property management must be designated to a specific management company.

The following details should be included in the property service agreement:

- The name and address of the management company.
- The name and registered office of the management company.
- Details of the designated apartment complex – the subject of the agreement.
- Particulars of the service to be provided under the agreement, including property management services and the provision of staff.
- The amount of fees payable and the procedure for collection (including non-payment).
- The period of the agreement.
- Details of professional indemnity insurance.

- Details of the records regarding the provision of services under the agreement.
- Complaints and redress procedures.
- Timetable for the delivery of services.
- Details of out-of-hours services.
- Reporting obligations of the management company.

Under section 58 of the Act, a management company must prepare and deliver an annual report, hold a meeting at least once a year, provide a detailed statement of all charges and make it available to the members at least twenty one days before the scheduled meeting, and provide a copy of the annual report at least ten days before the scheduled meeting. The meeting should take place within reasonable proximity of the apartment complex and at a reasonable time (this must be agreed by 75 per cent of the members). The proposed service charge must be rejected by at least 75 per cent of the members to be defeated. If this happens, the previous year's charges will apply, pending the adoption of a new service charge. If 60 per cent of the members agree to the charges at the meeting, the proposed service charges can be changed at that meeting.

If you are renting a home from your local authority there are two options:

- The Tenant Purchase Scheme (to be removed by the end of 2012) is available to tenants who have been renting for at least one year from their local authority. The rate to be paid is the difference between the current normal market value (of similar homes regardless if your home is worth more) less discounts (depending on the number of years you have been renting (3 per cent per year up to a maximum of 10 years)) plus €3,810. Stamp duty (as discussed earlier) is chargeable on all tenant purchase homes at a rate of €100. If you wish to sell the home within twenty years of your purchase, you must first get approval from the local authority. Mortgages for the purchase of the property are available from either the local authority or private financial providers

- The Incremental Purchase Scheme allows existing tenants who are tenants of the local authority, are renting through the Rental Accommodation Scheme (RAS) or are renting through approved bodies to buy new approved homes only (but not their own). The scheme allows for the full title of the new home to pass to the purchaser in return for 40–60 per cent of the all-in cost of the new property to be charged back to the purchaser at a declining rate of 2 per cent per year over a 20- or 30-year period. If the property is sold within the first five years, the full remaining charge is still applicable. If sold after that time the remaining amount due is owed to the local authority from the proceeds of the sale. The local authority or approved body has first preference if the owner wishes to sell. During that time, when the purchaser is paying back the local authority or approved body, the new purchaser is responsible for all the maintenance and ongoing 'private owner' costs and any major improvement works must be approved by the local authority in advance of the work taking place.

For further information contact your local authority or the Department of Environment, Community and Local Government (www.environ.ie).

I purchased a home under the Affordable Housing Scheme with assistance from my local authority, but I am now having structural problems. Who is responsible for the repair?

Essentially when buying a property under the Affordable Housing Scheme the agreement is between the buyer (you) and the seller. The seller is generally the builder and not the local authority. The local authority is not the 'land-lord' under these arrangements, nor is it the seller. The local authority simply facilitates the sale of the property at lower than market rates in accordance with approval of the application and in compliance with application criteria. Therefore any disputes should be taken up with the builder (see Chapter 2, Consumer Complaints, p. 81) or with the management company, if one is present (discussed later in this chapter). If sub-standard material was used in the building of these properties this is the responsibility of the builder and/or the local authority (under the building control regulations) if the development was not in compliance with best practice requirements.

I purchased a home under the Affordable Housing Scheme from my local authority, but I am now struggling to repay the mortgage. Is there any assistance for me?

It is advisable if you are having difficulty with your mortgage, and your loan is with your local authority, to discuss the matter as soon as possible with the local authority to try to arrange an alternative payment scheme. In addition, you should seek the assistance of MABS (www.mabs.ie).

In 2011, the Housing Finance Agency, which sets the mortgage rates for local authorities, decreased the rate from 3 per cent to 2.75 per cent. The Mortgage Protection Insurance Scheme rate for affordable housing buyers was also reduced and frozen for a five-year period. The Minister for Environment, Community and Local Government also announced that a new code of conduct for local authorities that provide mortgages to people under the Affordable Housing Scheme will be rolled out in 2012 providing similar support to that already in place for people who have mortgage difficulties with financial providers. At present, people in receipt of mortgages from local authorities cannot avail of the Mortgage Interest Supplement (MIS) scheme available to people in mortgage difficulties with financial institutions. This scheme, administered by the Department of Social Protection, can help people to pay a proportion of the interest of their mortgage if in financial difficulties, subject to a means test. In Budget 2012 the Minister announced that payment of the Mortgage Interest Supplement will be deferred for twelve months while a person in financial difficulties engages in the Mortgage Arrears Resolution Process (MARP).

Renting

I believe there are new regulations in the area of rented properties. What do these regulations mean?
Since 1 February 2009 new requirements are in place for accommodation rented after that date. In addition, since 1 January 2009 all homes for rent must have a Building Energy Rating (BER). The regulations do not apply to mobile or holiday homes, and other exempt buildings. Enforcement will be carried out by local city or county councils. Under the regulation, called Housing (Standards for Rented Houses) Regulations 2008 (SI 534/2008), properties must have:

- Structurally sound buildings (article 5).
- Self-contained bathroom facilities (article 6).

- Controllable heating (article 7).
- Space for food preparation, storage and laundry (article 8).
- Ventilation (article 9).
- Adequate lighting (including emergency lighting) (article 10).
- Fire safety (including a mains-wired smoke alarm) (article 11).
- Refuse facilities (communal area) (article 12).
- Electricity and/or gas (article 13).

Rental Accommodation Scheme

I have been renting privately for two years and receiving Rent Supplement. My application for local authority housing was submitted three years ago. I don't know how much longer it will be before I am given a council house. Are there any other supports available to me?

A scheme called the Rental Accommodation Scheme (RAS) was announced in July 2004. Under the new programme, local authorities will progressively assume responsibility for accommodating Rent Supplement recipients with long-term housing needs. The initial project to transfer existing recipients of eighteen months or more continuous duration is ongoing. Under this scheme, local authorities will enter into contracts with accommodation providers (landlords) to secure medium- to long-term availability of rented accommodation that meets minimum standards. Rent levels will be determined by negotiation between the landlord and the local authority, and the landlord must be tax compliant, registered with the Private Residential Tenancies Board (PRTB) and comply with the Residential Tenancies Act 2004 (landlord and tenant relationship). The tenant will therefore only pay normal local authority 'differential' rents (this rate may vary slightly between local authorities or approved bodies). Under Budget 2009, an additional €39.5 million was allocated to this programme. In Budget 2012 an additional €10 million was assigned to allow transfers into the Rental Accommodation Scheme.

Any disputes between the landlord and tenant may be resolved by the PRTB. Properties being used for the Rental Accommodation Scheme (RAS) are exempt from the non-principal private residence charge (€200 per annum).

The Social Welfare and Pensions 2007 Act now allows people who are on the waiting list and approved for the RAS to commence full-time employment (presuming they were unemployed for the previous twelve months and receiving Rent Supplement) and still be eligible to continue to receive Rent Supplement. Such provision (continuation of payment of Rent Supplement) is also applicable to people taking part in Community Employment or Back to Enterprise schemes (on a tapered basis). RAS housing will certainly be one of your offers from your local authority in relation to meeting your social housing (local authority) needs.

The Minister for the Department of Environment, Community and Local Government announced in December 2011 that 2,000 housing units will be made available to local authorities or approved bodies on a leasing basis from the National Asset Management Agency (NAMA) for people on social housing lists.

For further information check www.environ.ie or contact your local authority (city council or county council).

Landlord and Tenant Rights

I am a new tenant in a rented property. What are my rights and obligations as a tenant, and what are the rights and obligations of my landlord? Is there a need for the landlord to register the tenancy?

Firstly we must determine what type of tenancy you have entered. The three main types are periodic tenancy, fixed-term tenancy and a Part 4 tenancy. A periodic tenancy is a non-fixed period tenancy (generally a verbal agreement) running in line with the rent periods, i.e. weekly or monthly. So if you pay rent weekly or monthly–and you do not have any written agreement and have been renting for less than six months, the notice period may vary as per your verbal agreement but be no greater than four weeks (twenty-eight days). A fixed-term tenancy (or lease) is for a defined period of time, and you may not be able to 'break' this lease even if you provide advance notice in writing to your landlord regardless of the period (and therefore you may lose your deposit). If in this case you plan to leave it may be your obligation to seek a new tenant for the remaining period of the contract. If your landlord refuses to accept this new tenant, this may allow you to seek your deposit back from your landlord (due to breach of agreement). You can convert a fixed-term tenancy to a Part 4 tenancy by notifying your landlord between three and one months prior to the termination of your fixed-term tenancy. If you have been renting for six months and have not received any written agreement you automatically acquire a Part 4 tenancy. A Part 4 tenancy provides you with specific rights and obligations. The Residential Tenancies Act 2004 sets out these rights and obligations for both landlords and tenants under the Part 4 tenancy.

The tables below summarise these:

Tenant's Rights	Tenant's Obligations
To peaceful and exclusive occupation (restricted access of landlord)	To pay the rent and other charges due on time, and make the rent book available to the landlord (Housing (Miscellaneous Provisions) Act 1992)
To have contact details for landlord or agent	To notify the landlord of any repairs required and allow access to the property. Ensure the landlord (through non-action or omission) is not in breach of the Standards for Rented Houses, 1993
To refund of reasonable expenses after repair, for which the landlord was liable (advisable to discuss in advance)	Not to engage in or allow anti-social behaviour
To prompt return of deposit (subject to arrears or excessive wear and tear)	Not to sub-let (let to others) or change the use of the dwelling (residential to business) without the landlord's written consent
To be made aware of management fees and charges in relation to the dwelling	To inform the landlord of the identity of occupants who are resident in the dwelling
To refer dispute (to PRTB) without being penalised	To notify the landlord between 1 and 3 months before the end of the 6 month period of the intention to remain and the rights related (Part 4 of Act), i.e. extension of a further 3½ years

To be able to access registration details forwarded by landlord to PRTB	To provide the landlord with information to register the tenancy

Landlord's Rights	Landlord's Obligations
To refer disputes about a tenancy to the PRTB (presumed registered)	To register the tenancy with the PRTB
To review the rent annually (subject to maximum market rents)	To charge a rate that does not exceed market rates
To receive valid notice of termination from tenant when moving	To provide the tenant with 28 days' notice of any rent review or increase (dispute may be referred to the PRTB)
To terminate a tenancy before 6 months without a reason or after 6 months on specified grounds	To serve the tenant with a valid notice of termination
To recover possession without notice if tenant has vacated premises and rent is at least 28 days in arrears	To repair and maintain the structure of the premises (must comply with minimum standards – Housing (Miscellaneous Provisions) Act 1992)
To be informed of repairs required and allowed access (by appointment) to repair	To repair and maintain the inside of a dwelling to the standard at the start of the tenancy
To receive correct rent on due date	To return any deposit due (unless in arrears or if there is damage to dwelling)

To be informed of anyone residing in the premises (excluding casual guests) and to decide to allow tenant to sub-let or change use of dwelling	To provide the tenant with information regarding any agents acting on behalf of the landlord and give them contact details
To recover costs of repair from tenant if tenant's fault	To repay tenants for expenses of repair that should have been carried out by the landlord
	To provide tenants with a rent book and record transactions (Housing (Miscellaneous Provisions) Act 1992)
	To allow the tenant peaceful and exclusive enjoyment of the property and ensure compliance with the Equal Status Act 2004 (as amended)

Tenancies must be registered (excluding where the landlord is also resident in the home). Breach of registration may result in a €3,000 fine and/or six months in prison, along with a daily fine of €250 for a continuing offence.

The registration of a tenancy requires the completion of the PRTB1 form, providing the following:

- Address of dwelling.
- Name, address and Personal Public Service (PPS) number of both landlord or agent and tenants.
- Number of occupants.
- Description of dwelling (number of bed spaces), start date of tenancy and rent amount and frequency of payment.

Any changes in information must be updated with the PRTB, i.e. change in rent and tenancies. The Residential Tenancies (Amendment) Bill, due for completion in late 2012, proposes to reduce delays in the PRTB by streamlining and simplifying the Residential Tenancies Acts and to bring tenancies in the voluntary and cooperative housing sector within the remit of the Residential Tenancies Acts. The Bill will also amalgamate the PRTB and the Rent Tribunal. A new Landlord and Tenant Bill (due in late 2012 or early 2013) proposes to implement the Law Reform Commission's *Report on the Law of Landlord and Tenant* and reform and consolidate the general law on landlords and tenants. The Housing Bill proposes to provide for the rationalisation of housing agencies and to strengthen the regulatory framework for social housing as well as provide a statutory framework and regulation for a new scheme of Housing Assistance Payments. In addition, the new Housing (Miscellaneous Provisions) Act 2009 extended the role of the PRTB. These additional powers include disclosure of information contained in the register to the Revenue Commissioners.

I have been renting for nine months with my landlord and am planning on leaving. What notice must I give my landlord?
The following notice periods apply from landlords to tenants and tenants to landlords.

Seven days' notice can be given by a landlord where serious anti-social behaviour occurred, or potential serious risk to the dwelling and property by the tenant may occur or has occurred. In return, the tenant can give seven days' notice to the landlord where the behaviour of the landlord has caused a serious or immediate danger to the

life and limb of the tenant or even possible danger to the
structure of the property.

Duration of Tenancy (Minimum)	Notice Period from Tenant	Notice Period from Landlord
Less than 6 months	28 days (min.) 70 days (max.)	28 days (min.) 70 days (max.)
Greater than 6 months but less than a year	35 days	35 days
1–2 years	42 days	42 days
2–3 years	56 days	56 days
3–4 years	56 days	84 days
4 years or more	56 days	112 days

*How should I inform the landlord of my notice period – by
phone or in writing?*
Notice either from landlord to tenant or from tenant to
landlord requires the following:

Notice From Tenant	Notice From Landlord
Must be in writing	Must be in writing
Must be signed by the tenant	Must be signed by the landlord or agent
Must be dated with the day issued or served	Must be dated with the day issued or served
No reason is required for quitting	Reason must be given if tenancy is greater than 6 months
The date of termination must be specified (up to and before midnight on the day in question)	The date of termination must be specified (up to and before midnight on the day in question)

Must include a statement that any issues regarding the notice must be referred to the PRTB within 28 days of receipt of notice	Must include a statement that any issues regarding the notice must be referred to the PRTB within 28 days of receipt of notice

Notice should be served (in the case of a tenant) in person to the landlord or agent (receipt may assist confirmation), or left or posted to the landlord's or agent's contact address. It may be advisable, if posting, to send by registered post.

In cases of notice by a landlord, it should be handed in in person, left at the rented dwelling or posted. If the tenant is not present, it may be left in a reasonably obvious position outside the dwelling. Alternatively, if posting, it may be advisable to send by registered post for confirmation of delivery.

My landlord has given me notice to quit after twelve months. I feel I have the right to remain for a further three years. What valid reasons can the landlord give to quit?
The valid reasons a landlord can give in relation to notice to quit are:

- The tenant has failed to comply with the tenancy agreement (tenant must be given opportunity to resolve this).
- The landlord intends to sell the premises within the next three months.
- The landlord requires the dwelling for his own family occupation (you have the offer of first refusal if the dwelling becomes re-available).

- Substantial refurbishment is required and therefore the dwelling is required to be vacant (you have the offer of first refusal if the dwelling becomes re-available).
- The landlord intends to change the use of the dwelling (you have the offer of first refusal if the dwelling becomes re-available).

What exactly is antisocial behaviour?

Antisocial behaviour is activity that causes an offence, danger, injury, damage or loss, violence, bullying and harassment. It also includes continuous and persistent behaviour that prevents neighbours (in proximity) from peaceful residency.

I have given proper notice to leave and my landlord will not refund me my deposit. I am not sure if he is registered. What can I do?

Assuming you complied with proper notice requirements and procedures, and no damage was done to the property (beyond normal wear and tear), your landlord should provide you with your deposit upon departure. Tenants can refer disputes to the PRTB, even if the landlord has not registered the tenancy. However, landlords cannot refer disputes without prior registration. The person submitting the dispute will have to pay a €25 fee. Disputes regarding 'key' money or deposits where a tenancy never commenced will have to be referred to the Small Claims Court as this is not covered under the remit of the PRTB.

Dispute resolution may involve mediation or adjudication, as chosen by the parties, and/or a public hearing. Legal representation is not necessarily required by either party (legal costs are generally not covered in any award), as the dispute procedure is generally informal and open to all.

In some cases awards (up to the maximum of €60,000 in rent arrears awards) may be granted. If such awards are not complied with, they can be enforced by the Circuit Court. Awards for greater amounts will have to go through the normal court procedures.

I have not paid my rent for the last two months and my landlord has given me two weeks' notice to leave. Can he do this?
No, a landlord is required to give you written notification of arrears, as well as a period of two weeks' notice to pay the arrears. If you do not pay the arrears within the two-week period the landlord must then give you written notification of 28 days' notice to vacate the premises on grounds of breach of contract. Of course the written notification must be signed by the landlord, must be dated and served and must clearly state the termination date. In addition, the notification must include a statement referring any disputes to the PRTB within 28 days of the notice. If a case is referred to the PRTB for investigation, no further action by either party can take place.

I am renting a room in a friend's house. Am I a tenant, and do I have the same rights?
If you rent a room and share a house with your friend (landlord), you are not protected under the rights of the Residential Tenancies Act 2004. It would be advisable to have some written agreement between the parties (you and your friend) in case of difficulties, or if you wish to leave, for example, stating how much notice you should give.

My landlord wants to increase the rent. Can he do this and, if so, by how much?

The landlord cannot charge rent above the normal market rates. Rent reviews (or increases) can only take place once a year. In addition, a tenant can seek a rent review (annually). The landlord must give 28 days' notice in writing prior to the increase taking effect. Section 19 of the Residential Tenancies Act 2004 states the market rate is defined as 'the rent a non-sitting tenant would give and a willing landlord would take'. If there is a dispute regarding the rent review, either party can submit an application to the PRTB at least prior to the expiry of the 28-day notice, or at least prior to the proposed increase taking effect.

Management Companies

I believe the rules changed last year in relation to management companies. What does this mean for me?

The Multi-Unit Developments Act 2011 (which came into effect on 1 April 2011) contains detailed provisions concerning the management and operation of owners' management companies, including rules relating to the holding of annual general meetings, the calculation of service charges, the establishment of sinking funds (A sinking fund is money put aside every year to cover the cost of major long-term expenses.) and the making of house rules. The legislation will apply to multi-unit developments containing residential units only and to mixed-use developments containing residential units. It will also apply to housing estates which have owners' management companies. Where no sinking fund has been established, such a fund must be put in place within eighteen months, i.e. by 30 September 2011 at the latest.

Prior to this Act, within the Housing (Miscellaneous Provisions) Act 1992 tenants had specific rights in relation to being made aware of management companies and ensuring any complaints via the landlord are formally replied to (in writing).

The Multi-Unit Developments Act 2011 requires that the common areas be transferred to the management company prior to sale of the first residential unit. In existing developments in which a residential unit has already been sold but the common areas have not been transferred by the developer to the management company, the transfer must have been made within six months, i.e. before 30 September 2011.

The Property Services (Regulatory) Act 2011 provides for the establishment of a Property Services Regulatory Authority and to give effect to the *Report of the Auctioneering/Estate Agency Review Group*. Management agents, i.e. companies that manage properties on behalf of landlords, will also be covered by this authority. This now means that all property service providers must be registered and licensed to operate. If these requirements are breached offences can be punishable by a fine or imprisonment. The property service provider must be tax compliant, ensure the licence is available for inspection and ensure it has professional indemnity for its work. Any complaints regarding a licensed property service provider can be made to the Regulatory Authority for investigation and/or mediation. If found guilty, claims can be appealed to the Property Service Appeal Board. Complaints or further information can be found by contacting the Property Services Regulatory Authority at 1890-252712 or check the website at www.npsra.ie.

For the purpose of clarity, the definition of a 'competent authority' is a property service provider, within the meaning of article 4 of Directive 2006/123/EC, which has functions in relation to persons who provide a service that substantially corresponds to a service which falls within the definition of 'property service'.

Will I have a say or a vote in any matter? What happens if I am not happy and have a dispute?

As regards voting rights in owners' management companies, the general rule for residential developments is that one vote attaches to each residential unit. In mixed-use developments, other voting arrangements may apply as long as they are fair and equitable. Voting rights will be transferred upon sale or purchase.

The Act establishes a new Circuit Court jurisdiction to deal with disputes between parties. However, if mediation or another form of dispute resolution has not already been attempted, the court may require the parties to engage in a mediation process. Costs may be awarded against a party which does not engage in a meaningful way in such mediation.

How will my service charge be calculated?

Section 18 (subsection 2) states any charge shall be approved by a general meeting of the members of the company, while subsection (3) outlines the categories of expenditure which must be itemised in the scheme of charges. Subsection (4) provides that in any case in which over 75 per cent of the members do not approve the proposed charge the existing charge shall remain in place until agreement on and adoption of a new charge. Subsection

(13) provides that the annual service charge must be calculated on a transparent and fair basis

Who will make the 'house rules'?

Section 23 provides that an owners' management company may make house rules for the effective operation and maintenance of the multi-unit development. The rules must be consistent with any covenants or conditions contained in the documents of title (subsection (2)) and have the objective of advancing the quiet enjoyment of the unit owners and achieving a fair balancing of the rights of such owners (subsection (3)).

House rules must be agreed by a meeting of members of the owners' management company (subsection (4)) and notice of such meeting must be given to members at least 21 days before the meeting together with a copy of the draft rules (subsections (5) and (6)). When house rules are made, a copy shall be given to unit owners by the owners' management company (subsection (7)). Subsection (8) provides that the owners' management company can make the initial house rules for the development prior to the sale of the first residential unit. Subsection (9) provides that house rules may be amended in the same manner as they are made. Where a unit is let, it shall be a term of the letting that it is subject to the observance of the rules by the tenants (subsection (10)).

Our management company has clamping around our apartment block. Can they do this?

Essentially the rules and regulations of the management company are defined in the house rules (as mentioned above). Clamping by management companies can be possible if the area is a private area and not a public area. It is the responsibility of the local authority (via bylaws and the allocation and charging of paid parking areas) or the Gardaí to fine, clamp or remove vehicles causing obstructions in public areas. Clamping of vehicles is authorised by the Road Traffic (Immobilisation of Vehicles) Regulations 1998 and the Road Traffic (Removal, Storage and Disposal of Vehicles) Regulations 1983–1991 giving power to local authorities to tow away vehicles that have been illegally parked and are causing serious congestion. There is no regulation in relation to clamping and fees in or on private areas. The new Vehicle Immobilisation Regulation Bill proposes to provide for regulation of the private clamping industry.

Can we set up our own management company?

Yes, 'owners' management company' means a company established under the Companies Acts for the purpose of becoming the owner of the common areas of a multi-unit development and for managing, maintaining and repairing such areas. For the purposes of imposing certain requirements of the Acts on existing owners' management bodies which are not companies, subsection (3) provides that reference to an 'owners' management company' shall include reference to an industrial and provident society, a partnership or unincorporated body, or a group of persons who own the common areas of a multi-unit development

What if our previous management company was struck off?

Section 30 addresses the problems which arise when an owners' management company is struck off the Companies Register for non-compliance with reporting requirements. It provides for an extended period during which such a company may be restored to the Register. At present, a company that has been struck off has a period of one year within which to provide the Registrar with the relevant information and accounts. Thereafter application for restoration must be made in the High Court. Section 30 provides that the period of one year is extended to six years in the case of owners' management companies. When restored to the Register, it shall be deemed to have continued in existence as if it had never been struck off. Each application for restoration must be accompanied by a certificate from a solicitor or accountant to the effect that the company is operating as an owners' management company.

SUMMARY CHECKLIST: Management Companies

When you buy an apartment, it is one 'vote' for each unit. ☐

When buying an apartment, you never own the property 'freehold' (unlike a house); you have a 'leasehold'. It is important to find out how long the period is for. ☐

Have you seen, or are you aware of the memorandum and articles of association of the management company? These documents refer to the legal set-up of a company, and how it is meant to run. ☐

When was the last annual general meeting (AGM)? You may wish to contact the Office of the Director of Corporate Enforcement (ODCE) if no AGM has been held. ☐

How much is your proposed 'service charge' in your lease? Will it increase next year and by how much? Was the new service charge approved? Have you seen detailed financial statements/costs? There may be interest/penalty on unpaid service charges. ☐

Check with the Companies Registration Office (www.cro.ie) to see who the directors of the management company are, if it is registered and when the last company returns were made. If the regulations were not complied with, this could potentially cause difficulties if you want to sell. ☐

Has the management company employed a management agent or property service provider to carry out the day-to-day activities? Are they licensed and approved? ☐

Has the developer released the title to the property? If not, s/he may have control, and potentially prevent the title being passed to the city/county council. (No time limit exists.) ☐

Make sure to check the contract of sale or tenancy to be fully aware of the possibility of removing or replacing a management company. ☐

Seek legal opinion in the management and/or removal of management companies. ☐

If you are a tenant, who pays the service charge – you or the landlord? If there are disputes in relation to payments, service may be affected. ☐

Ensure all requests for repair or complaints are fully investigated, resolved and communicated back to you, the tenant or buyer, within a reasonable period of time. ☐

Who makes the house rules? ☐

Is there an adequate 'sinking' fund? ☐

If you are unhappy with the running of the management company, look to call an EGM (extraordinary general meeting). ☐

For further information contact the Private Residential Tenancies Board (PRTB) at 01-6350600 (www.prtb.ie); Threshold (www.threshold.ie) at 01-6353651 (Dublin), 091-563080 (Galway) or 021-4278848 (Cork); or the National Consumer Agency (www.nca.ie) at 1890-432432.

Energy Rating and Insulation

I am selling my home. I believe I have to have it 'energy rated' before I can sell. Is this true?
Since 1 January 2009 all homes (including second-hand homes) for sale require a Building Energy Rating (BER)

under the European Communities (Energy Performance of Buildings) Regulations 2006. The BER shows how energy-efficient a building is. The system has been in operation for new houses since 2007. The label rating (A–G) is similar to electrical appliance rating: 'A' rated homes are most efficient, and those rated 'G' are least efficient. The certificate is valid for ten years. Fines of up to €5,000 are in place for non-compliance with the regulations. The BER can only be carried out by registered assessors (available from www.sei.ie/ber).

Heating Costs

I am looking to get some work done on my home to cut down on my heating costs. Are there any grants available? An insulation programme (Home Energy Savings Scheme) offers grant aid of between €200 and €3,600 for home improvements and is available to owners and landlords of homes built before 2006. The minimum grant application is €400 (which must exclude the Building Energy Rating (BER) assessment grant of €50). A BER assessment must be carried out both before the work commences and after the work has been completed. The largest single grant is a €3,600 contribution to work on external cavity wall insulation, and grants for €320 to €2,000 for internal wall insulation are also available. Since December 2011 internal and external wall insulation grants will no longer be granted separately but rather based on the house type. Between €400 and €560 will be available towards heating control upgrades. €800 is available towards solar panels (previously administered under the Greener Home Scheme). Works completed by contractors on their own homes are only allowable for the cost of materials and not labour. Applications must be made and approved before any work commences, and the grant payment will be only be made after the work has been completed by a registered Sustainable Energy Authority of Ireland (SEAI) contractor. If the total cost of the work (including VAT) is less than the maximum grant value only the actual cost amount will be granted.

The Warmer Home Scheme aimed to improve the energy efficiency and warmth of homes lived in by people on a low income (essentially people on the Fuel Allowance Scheme) and for owner-occupiers of homes built prior to 2002. As part of this scheme, minor works are carried out in people's homes (for a small or no fee), including the provision of attic insulation, draught proofing, lagging jackets and cavity wall insulation. The Greener Home Scheme provided grants to homeowners (for the cost of the equipment only) to buy a home heating system that uses a renewable energy source, including solar power, heat pumps and biomass. Grants of up to €3,500 were available to homeowners for homes occupied prior to June 2008 that had existing heating systems and where the new system was installed by a recognised and qualified installer.

A new national upgrade programme called Better Energy Homes Scheme was launched in May 2011. The Home Energy Saving Scheme, Warmer Homes Scheme and Greener Home Scheme were merged into the Better Energy Homes Scheme at that time. For further information contact Better Energy Homes Scheme (www.seai.ie or Lo-Call 1850-927000).

Budget 2011 introduced a tax relief at the standard rate of tax for improvements to your home (homeowners only, excluding landlords) to promote energy efficiency. The maximum relief is €10,000 per applicant or €15,000 per household and the tax credit (20 per cent) will be granted in the following tax year (2012 onwards). The commencement order to put this into operation (section 13 of the Finance Act 2011) has not been signed and therefore this scheme is not operational as of yet.

The Household Charge

I have heard property taxes will be introduced? When will these new charges take effect?
In the EU/IMF Programme of Financial Support for Ireland (1 December 2010) it is stated that a property tax is to be implemented in Budget 2012, with further increases in charges in Budget 2013. In Budget 2012 a new Household Charge (under the Local Government (Household Charge) Act 2011) of €100 per permanent dwelling (excluding vessels and mobile homes not permanently attached to the ground but including flats, apartments and bedsits) was introduced. The €100 fee is chargeable to homeowners (and people who have leased property for over twenty years) and landlords (not tenants) and if jointly owned both parties are equally liable.

Arrangements are in place to allow the payment of the €100 fee in one lump sum or in four instalments (for 2012 on 13 March 2012, 14 May 2012, 13 July 2012 and 10 September 2012). If you wish to pay by instalments you must register and set up your direct debit by 29 February 2012. If you wish to pay in one lump sum you must do so by 31 March each year. The payment is due since 1 January 2012 and late payments up to six months will be liable to a late payment fee of 10 per cent of the amount outstanding. Late payments will be liable to a 20 per cent late payment fee on the amount outstanding on payments between six to twelve months overdue, and 30 per cent on payments delayed over twelve months. Interest is chargeable at 1 per cent per month. This payment will be collected on a self-declared basis and there is an obligation on all individuals (even those entitled to a waiver) to apply online at www.householdcharge.ie, or submit their application to their local authority by 31 March 2012, or post their application form to Household Government Management Agency, PO Box 12168, Dublin 1. Those eligible to a waiver will be granted one upon approval of their application. Information and data held by Government bodies and semi-state bodies, e.g. the Department of Social Protection, Revenue Commissioners, PRTB and ESB, may be shared with each corresponding local authority in relation to the property. Local authorities have the power to prosecute people who do not pay.

Unpaid charges will remain a lien on the property and if selling your property you will need to present a certificate of discharge proving payment. If you die and you have not paid the charge prior to death, your personal representative (responsible for administering your estate) will be required to pay outstanding charges due within three months of the date of submission of the grant of representation. If payment is not paid during this time, interest and charges continue from the date of submission of the grant of representation. A fully assessed value-based property tax will be implemented in 2013, replacing the €100 flat fee.

Who is liable for the Household Charge and do I have to pay if I have more than one home?
All persons (including joint owners although only one owner's PPS number is required for the form) who own

residential property, including apartments and bedsits, resided in as at 1 January 2012 are liable for the Household Charge of €100 per property, which was due on 31 March 2012 under the Local Government (Household Charge) Act 2011.

I am selling my home at present am I liable for the charge?
Yes, the important date is 1 January 2012. If you were resident in the premises as of that date, you are still liable for the charge.

I bought a home on 25 January 2012. Am I liable for the Household Charge on this home?
No, you would not be liable for the Household Charge as you were not resident at the new address as of 1 January 2012, but you may be liable for the charge on a previous address resided at as of 1 January 2012.

Who is exempt from charge?
Those residing in mobile homes and those in local authority housing, housing associations or cooperatives are exempt. Property owned by government departments of the HSE, voluntary housing bodies, trust or approved bodies and shared ownerships are also exempt.

In addition, people who have been in long-term care for over a year (prior to 1 January 2012) due to medical reasons or physical infirmity (which must be certified) do not have to pay the charge. These exempt properties do not need to be registered but proof may be sought as to why.

Who can claim a waiver?
If you were in receipt of Mortgage Interest Supplement as at 1 January 2012, you are not liable for the charge and

must register for a waiver. This also applies to those living in unfinished housing estates. The list of qualifying estates is on the www.householdcharge.ie website.

What are the penalty rates for late payment?
The penalty rate is €16 if the charge is not paid within six months of 31 March 2012 for 2012 charges (10 per cent fee and 1 per cent interest per month), up to €32 if not paid within twelve months from 31 March 2012 for 2012 charges (20 per cent fee and 1 per cent interest per month), and over €42 if paid later than twelve months from 31 March 2012 for 2012 charges (30 per cent fee and 1 per cent interest per month). The charge will remain on a property for up to twelve years.

How can the payment be made?
Payments could be made in person at your local authority office before 31 March 2012 only. Alternatively, payment can be made online at www.householdcharge.ie or by cheque, postal order or bank draft by post to Local Government Management Agency, PO Box 12168, Dublin 1.

If I am selling my home what proof do I need that the Household Charge has been paid?
Upon payment you will receive proof of payment. This will be required if you wish to sell. Alternatively, a certificate of discharge may be requested to prove payment has been made.

What happens the Household Charge after someone dies?
Essentially, any outstanding Household Charge is due within three months of commencing probate. If the

payment is not made within the three-month window, additional charges will apply on top of any existing payment due.

The charge remains on the property for a maximum of twelve years. Local authorities can seek to collect the charge through through court or outsource the debt collection to a local government services board (section 13 of the Local Government (Household Charge) Act 2011). Summary proceeds for an offence must be instituted not later than two years after the local authority forms an opinion justifying an offence (section 15). Court fines can include all relevant expenses incurred by the local authority on a case-by-case basis and fines of up to €2,500 may be imposed (class C fine). Further fines of €100 per day may be imposed if further breaches occur.

Why have I not received a bill/invoice?

The Household Charge is a self-assessment charge; therefore, people need to register their property for the charge (or waiver) to be billed/invoiced in the future. The Act allows for data sharing between the DSP, Revenue Commissioners, PRTB and ESB (section 14).

Second Home Charge (Non-Principal Private Residence (NPPR))

I have a second home; will I have the pay the second home charge and the Household Charge?

Yes, unfortunately both charges will apply. The NPPR charge (€200 per property) is applicable to people who have second or subsequent properties or holiday homes, even if they are renting them out (the 'Rent-a-Room' scheme and situations where the landlord resides in the property are exempt). Properties being rented out under the RAS (Rental Accommodation Scheme) were previously exempt under the charge but are now applicable since the passing of the Local Government (Household Charge) Act 2011. The charge is also applicable to people who have properties in Ireland but who do not reside here. The liability date is 31 March each year and payment must be made by 30 June. A late fee of €20 per month is chargeable from June onwards for late payments. Fees paid in person over the counter to the local authority (since 1 January 2012) impose a handling fee (which must not be greater than the reasonable cost of providing the service – section 19(h4) of the Local Government (Household Charge) Act 2011). Accounts can be registered and paid online at www.nppr. ie. If you are registering in person or by application form you must do so with the local authority in which the second property is, and not your own local authority. This payment is a self-assessment tax and you are responsible for your own registration. People can apply for an exemption, upon registration or renewal to their relevant local authority.

Exemptions to the charge are:

- If the second property is a granny flat for which you are not receiving any rent, or the person living there is a family member, they are your legal guardian or the person is under a ward of court, and the property is within 2km of your home.
- If you are moving home, if you move from the first property (your main residence) into the second property not later than six months after 31 March you can get a refund of the charge as long as you no longer own the first property. If you purchase a new property but have not moved

into it within six months of 31 March and you still own your first property, you are liable for the fee. The fee is due even though it is part of a 'moving' process.

- If you are separated or divorced and have a financial interest in a second property.
- Homes owned by charities or certain trusts.
- If you move into a nursing home.
- If it is a caravan or mobile home (not permanently attached to the ground – as amended by section 19(2b) Local Government (Household Charge) Act 2011).

Water Charges

It is proposed that water charges will be introduced in 2012–2013. This new water charge will occur after the transfer of water services from the local authorities to a water utility provider. There is as yet no indication as to when this transfer will take place but it is likely to be either 2012 or 2013.

Neighbourhood Nuisance

My neighbour plays music excessively loudly late at night. I have contacted the Gardaí but they have not done anything. What can I do?
Firstly, it would be advisable to try to discuss the issue with your neighbour and try to come to an amicable agreement. Nuisance, public or private, is generally described as unreasonable interference with a person's right to enjoyment of property, as would be expected by an ordinary person. Public nuisance is generally when three or more residents are affected by the nuisance and report such incidents. If discussions with your neighbour are unsuccessful,

it may be advisable to contact your local authority environmental officer or take a case to the local District Court.

An application can be taken to the District Court, for a small fee, under the Environmental Protection Agency Act 1992, (Noise) Regulations 1994 to seek abatement (termination/ceasing of the noise). This action can be taken without legal representation being required and a court hearing date will be set for the investigation. It is therefore advisable to keep full records of incidents or correspondence to support your application. The court may request the noise be reduced, restricted or stopped completely. Fines of up to €3,000 or twelve months' imprisonment may be enforced. Since 1 January 2007, anti-social behaviour orders (ASBOs) have been put in place for adults. In such cases the Gardaí may issue a behaviour warning (valid for three months) to prevent such behaviour. If a warning is breached, a behaviour order (by the courts) may be granted. Breaches of behaviour orders may incur a fine of up to €3,000 or six months' imprisonment. The proposed Noise Nuisance Bill intends to bring into effect comprehensive legislation to address noise pollution, which includes noisy parties, noisy 'adapted' vehicles and continuously sounding alarms. The noise level for cars is proposed to be 74 decibels and 80 decibels for large vehicles. The Noise Nuisance Bill also proposes to give powers to both the local authority and Gardaí to enter premises and remove noise equipment and issue on-the-spot fines. In addition, mediation may be required or directed between neighbours to resolve disputes. The primary time frame for noise nuisance will be between the hours of 11 p.m. and 7 a.m. In addition, the Gardaí will have powers to disconnect house alarms and tow away vehicles if they are causing a nuisance due to noise. Noise from road, rail and air traffic is covered separately under EU Directive 2002/49/EC and is not covered under domestic noise.

My neighbour's dog barks all night and makes it difficult for me to sleep. What can I do?
Similar to the previous question, it would be advisable to discuss the matter with your neighbour and try to come to an amicable arrangement. If this is not possible, you can contact your local authority environmental officer, with specific reference to the Control of Dogs Acts 1986–1992. They may be able to remedy the situation with your neighbour.

As above, an application can be taken to the District Court, for a small fee, under the Environmental Protection Agency Act 1992, (Noise) Regulations 1994 to seek abatement (termination). This action can be taken without legal representation being required and a court hearing date will be set for investigation. It is therefore advisable to keep full records of incidents and correspondence to support your application. You must inform your neighbour of your intention to submit an application to court by firstly notifying them through the provision and timely delivery of a special notice form available from your local authority. The court may request the noise be reduced, restricted or stopped completely. Fines of up to €3,000 or twelve months' imprisonment may be enforced.

Alternatively, if you feel the animal is being ill-treated you may wish to contact the Irish Society for Prevention of Cruelty to Animals (ISPCA) for further assistance. The Dog Breeding Establishments Act 2010 in particular provides for the regulation and registration of dog breeding (to be administered and managed by local authorities). The Animal Health and Welfare Bill also proposes to consolidate responsibility for the welfare of all animals. The Veterinary (Amendment) Bill proposes to enable persons other than veterinary practitioners and veterinary nurses to carry out certain procedures on or in relation to animals.

My neighbour's alarm is continually going off for periods of up to 45 minutes at a time. Is there anything I can do? It's driving me crazy!
A standard for intruder alarms has been set across Europe since September 2003. The new standard ensures stricter controls around the minimum and maximum duration of an alarm going off. The minimum is 90 seconds and the maximum is fifteen minutes. This rule only applies to new alarms fitted since September 2003. Alarms fitted prior to this date have a greater minimum and maximum limit.

The same procedure should be taken for noise pollution (nuisance) from neighbours as described above. You should try to discuss the issue with your neighbour and inform them of your concerns. There may simply be a technical adjustment required to resolve the problem.

If the nuisance continues over a period of time without resolution, you can contact your local authority or the District Court to request taking out an application under the Environmental Protection Act (a small fee will apply). No legal representation is necessarily required (but you are not excluded from availing of it at your own expense). A court date will be set for the hearing and all facts will be fully investigated. Restrictions on future noise or noise levels may apply. Fines of up to €3,000 and/or twelve months' imprisonment can be set.

In other situations, direct action may need to be taken to stop the nuisance. It is essential in such cases to seek legal advice and/or discuss the problem with the Gardaí. The Noise Nuisance Bill intends to bring into effect comprehensive legislation to address noise pollution, specifically continuously sounding alarms. In addition, it is also an offence for a house alarm to be fitted by a non-licensed provider. Under section 37 of the Private Security Services Act 2004, unlicensed suppliers can be prosecuted, fined and/or imprisoned for breach of compliance with the Act. The Private Security Authority is the statutory body with responsibility for licensing and regulating the private security industry (including security guards and door supervisors (bouncers)).

Are there any alternatives to resolving neighbourhood disputes without going to court?
Yes, community mediation is an alternative method of resolution. Mediation is when both parties agree to meet with a neutral party to try to resolve their difficulty. Community mediation will not take place if legal proceedings have already commenced. Mediated agreements can be either verbal or written agreements. Community mediation is generally a free service. In addition, since 1 January 2010 new Circuit Court rules (SI 539/2009) have come into place to allow for civil cases to be adjourned for up to 28 days to allow for parties to use mediation, conciliation and arbitration or any other dispute resolution method to settle proceedings. As well as this, the new Mediation Bill is proposed to provide for implementation of recommendations of the Law Reform Commission to assist with the provision of alternative dispute resolution options.

My neighbour's trees are overhanging our garden. What can I do?
It would be advisable to try to discuss the matter with your neighbour regarding maintenance of trees and a duty of care to maintain them to a reasonable standard. It may also be advisable to seek a copy of boundary drawings to confirm exactly where the boundary starts and finishes.

Where such overhanging branches are causing a nuisance, you may trim back all branches to the boundary. Any trimming of such branches on your neighbour's property may be seen as trespass. Any trimmings must be offered back to your neighbour before being disposed of, as such branches are your neighbour's property (if the tree is planted in your neighbour's property). The Land and Conveyancing Law Reform Act 2009 now enforces new rules to deal with disputes over walls and fences separating neighbours. This is designed to regulate the rights of owners in relation to repairs beside boundaries that are impossible to carry out without access to the neighbour's property. Such approval will be grantable through a request for a 'work order' from the District Court to allow access to a neighbour's property.

I live along the LUAS line and am concerned in relation to CCTV cameras overlooking my premises. What can I do?
The Privacy Bill proposes to clarify this area. The Bill provides a defence that CCTV in operation for the purpose of law, including the protection of persons and property, as well as the prevention and investigation of crime, is allowable. The Bill proposes a right of reasonable privacy with respect to the rights of others, public order and the common good. The Bill also takes into account the European Court of Human Rights. It restricts the use of

surveillance, harassment or 'undercover' recording unless it used for the purpose of public importance and is fair and reasonable. The recommended remedies could be injunction, damages or return of material, i.e. pictures, recordings, etc. All actions must be taken within one year of the incident (although this may be extended to two years on approval of the court). An alternative Privacy Bill is being proposed under Private Members Business in the Seanad (March 2012).

From time to time, my neighbour parks in front of my driveway. What can I do?
It would be advisable to discuss the matter with your neighbour and inform them that it is an offence to block access to your driveway. If the problem persists, you do have a right to contact your local Gardaí and lodge a formal complaint for investigation as it is a complaint under SI 182/1997 Road Traffic (Traffic and Parking) Regulations 1997 section 13(1) to drive along or across (wholly or partly) a footway and under section 36 (2)(g) 'in any place, position or manner that will result in the vehicle obstructing an entrance or an exit for vehicles to or from a premises, save with the consent of the occupier of such premises', or on a footway (section 36(2)(i)).

My mother is in her seventies, lives alone and is quite infirm. There are a number of children in the area annoying her on the green in front of her house. Is there anything I can do?
Firstly, it may be possible for her to seek assistance via the Senior Alerts Scheme, which replaced the Scheme of Community Support for Older People in 2010. Such schemes provide subsidised installation and monitoring

of pendant alarm systems and/or sensor lights for people aged 65 or over living alone and/or of limited income. The scheme also covers grants for smoke alarms or carbon monoxide alarms, and security equipment for windows and doors. Unfortunately, the scheme does not cover the cost of annual monitoring fees or intruder alarms. The pendant system automatically contacts a monitoring station if detached from the pendant. The monitoring station will then contact the next of kin (up to three persons) to inform them. Applications can be made through your local registered group or if not already registered groups can apply. A full list and applications are available from the Department of the Environment, Community and Local Government. Applications cannot be made on an individual basis and at all times the equipment remains the property of the registered group. For further details please contact 071-9186700 (www.environ.ie).

Secondly, with reference to daily supports, it may be advisable to contact her local public health nurse with reference to an assessment of her needs. Such needs (depending on assessment) may include the possibility of a home care package, home help assistance from the HSE and the possibility of 'meals on wheels'. Thirdly, with reference to her security, contact the local Neighbourhood Watch programme, run in conjunction with the Gardaí, regarding possible anti-social behaviour or contact the Gardaí directly in relation to such incidents and/or monitoring of the area. Anti-social behaviour orders (ASBOs) are in place since 1 March 2007 for children (aged twelve to eighteen) if they cause harassment, serious fear, intimidation, distress, persistent danger or serious impairment of the enjoyment of life or property. Prior to the order being set, the superintendent may meet with the parents (and/

or juvenile liaison officer (JLO)) to discuss such behaviour. A 'good behaviour' contract for six months may be drawn up and reviewed periodically over three-month periods. If this agreement is breached, the District Court may grant an ASBO. The ASBO may prevent specific children from doing certain activities. The ASBO may be valid for up to two years.

Trespassers

I am concerned regarding the safety of my property. What steps can I take to protect my land?
Trespassing occurs when someone deliberately or negligently enters land or a building without a lawful reason. Such trespassing can occur even when the land or building has been entered lawfully (for a reason), but the entrant has outstayed the legal period of time (trespass ab initio), e.g. loitering in the cinema when the film is over.

Reasonable force may be used for the protection of property, which is appropriate to the risk and situation.

The Occupiers' Liability Act 1995 sets down criteria specifically in relation to trespassing, stating the owner has a duty of care not to injure the trespasser intentionally and not to act with reckless disregard, i.e. act without prior thought of injury (section 4(1)). Reckless disregard must be assessed on a case-by-case basis taking into consideration numerous factors.

If the purpose of the trespasser is criminal and a criminal act has been committed, the duty of the owner is to not injure intentionally. The courts may assess each situation in light of its merits and in the interests of justice. The new Criminal Law (Defence and the Dwelling) Act 2011 amends existing legislation so that it applies to defence of the person and the person's home. The Act covers not just the person's home but the area around the home, but not a public place, i.e. public access free of charge. The new legislation states the use of 'justifiable force'. Justifiable force is defined as (section 2(b)):

- the force used is only such as is reasonable in the circumstances to protect himself or herself or another person present in the dwelling from injury, assault, detention or death caused by a criminal act,
- to protect his or her property or the property of another person from appropriation, destruction or damage caused by a criminal act to prevent the commission of a crime or to effect, or assist in effecting, a lawful arrest

The Act also considers whether there were reasonable grounds for the action (section 2(4)) although it is not relevant if the person using the force had a safe exit without having to use force (section 2(5)) and there is no obligation to retreat (section 3). A person may be acquitted of the crime if they acted under duress, the act was involuntary, the person was intoxicated (drink, drugs or substance abuse) or insane and not responsible for their acts (section 2(8)). This legislation amends the Non-Fatal Offences against the Person Act 1997.

I have a dog and am concerned he will attack a trespasser. Will I be liable?
The Control of Dogs Acts 1986–1992 impose a strict liability for any injury by a dog that either attacks a person or causes injury to livestock (section 21(1)). This is regardless of any previous indications (or lack thereof) that the

dog may have a propensity to mischievous or vicious behaviour.

The exception, which may apply, is in relation to trespassers onto land (section 21(3)) and in such cases you will only be liable if you were negligent (factors would need to be assessed) or caused the dog to attack the trespasser.

A dog may be shot (section 23) if it was worrying livestock or was in a place where livestock was injured or killed and it cannot be seized. Rules are also in place to restrict certain dogs in a public place and if so, they must be muzzled, have a strong collar with identifiable details of the dog and be controlled by a person aged sixteen or over (as under the Control of Dogs Regulations 1998 (SI 442/1998).

Occupier's Liability

I was recently in a shop when I slipped on a wet floor. The area was not sealed off. Is the shop owner liable for my injury?
The Occupiers' Liability Act 1995 clearly sets down three categories of entrants (persons) to premises and the liability to each. These are:

* Visitors – persons who enter premises with the express or implied permission (invited to/asked to) of the occupier.
* Recreation users – those who come on to the land for recreation purposes, e.g. people using football pitches (local authority).
* Trespassers.

In this situation, people shopping would be classified as 'visitors'. The duty owed to visitors is to take reasonable care and ensure such persons do not suffer injury or damage. Also, a visitor has a duty of care for their own safety and the care of others, e.g. children. Therefore, in assessing the situation, factors to consider are what a normal, reasonable person would do in the circumstances and what steps the occupier took or had taken with reference to maintenance of property and awareness of safety issues.

In some cases, the occupier can reduce their liability by displaying a visible notice (generally at the entrance to a premises) amending or excluding their duty to 'visitors'. Such notice by the occupier cannot reduce the level of care below a threshold of a duty not to injure an entrant or to act with reckless disregard (without care).

The injury I sustained in the shop as part of the fall has become more painful. My GP is sending me to a specialist. Who will cover my costs and what if there is long-term damage?

InjuriesBoard.ie (formerly known as the Personal Injuries Assessment Board (PIAB)) was set up to assist in the assessment of compensation claims for injuries at work, and motor and public liability accidents. It assists in reducing the time it takes to settle a claim and in reducing legal costs.

It is advisable for the claimant (person making claim) to inform the occupier (respondent) within two months of a claim. Since 31 March 2005 the time limit for making a claim is two years after the incident.

The application procedure includes completing an application form, including medical assessment, relevant receipts for financial loss, correspondence with the respondent (shop) and a fee of €45. The respondent (shop) has 90 days to make a decision after receiving a copy of the complaint.

If either the claimant or respondent rejects the assessment within a defined period of time (28 days), either party can pursue the issue in the courts upon the issue of an 'authorisation' document (legal document to approve further proceedings). The role of InjuriesBoard.ie is purely to assess the amount of compensation due. Such rates may be determined by the 'Book of Quantum' (rates book for compensation of injuries). The Personal Injuries Assessment Board (Amendment) Act 2007 states that if you reject an award by InjuriesBoard.ie and then take a case to court, and if the offer is lower than that previously offered, you are not entitled to legal costs.

For further details please contact 1890-829121 (www. injuriesboard.ie).

Flooding, Snow, Frost and Ice

Does my house insurance cover flooding? What contents are actually covered?
Yes, the majority of insurance policies cover flooding, unless there is an 'exclusion' clause in the policy (if your area is identified as a risk area). Policies tend to cover fire, flood and storm, burglary, fallen trees and so on, subject to your compliance with the policy (make sure your alarm is on and the premises is not vacant for more than 30 days). Items covered include any moveable objects, for example carpets. It is important to check if your policy covers 'new for old' or the value of the items after wear and tear. Vehicles are not covered under your house policy, so if they are damaged in a flood you would submit a claim under the vehicle insurance.

What does the 'excess' mean on my claim? What should I do to process my claim?

The 'excess' is the amount of money you must pay yourself. This will vary depending on your policy threshold. The excess affects the price of your insurance policy: the greater the coverage, the higher the premium. To process your claim contact your insurance company immediately after the damage is caused. It would be advisable to have photographic evidence of all damage. For large claims you may need an assessor, who you may have to pay privately.

How do I know if I am in a flood plain? How can I prepare for flooding in the future?

Check the website www.floodmaps.ie. This site will advise you if there have been any previous incidents on record in your area. Also be aware that many insurers will have a comprehensive list of flood risk areas from their audit. The guide *Flooding: Plan, Prepare, Protect* can be downloaded from www.flooding.ie.

Who is the regulatory body in charge of insurance companies? What steps should I take in future when looking for a policy?

Having exhausted your complaint with your insurance company you may wish to complain to the Financial Ombudsman. Since April 2005 the Insurance Ombudsman has been incorporated into the Financial Ombudsman role. When looking for a new policy, check:

- The value of all contents in your home (do not overestimate).
- Rebuilding costs and also identify items of greater value to be itemised on your policy.

- The excess rates and the policy details.
- Whether flooding is excluded on your policy.

How important is it to get the right valuation? What guidelines should be taken?
If you undervalue your items, this may reduce your claim and put you at a financial loss. If you overvalue your contents, your claim may not be honoured as it is not the real and actual market value of the items damaged. When calculating the cost of rebuilding for your policy do not use the current market value of your home. Instead estimate the physical 'rebuild' cost (check the Society of Chartered Surveyors' website for guidelines: www.scs.ie).

For further information on policies and premiums contact the Financial Regulator at 1890-777777, or check the website www.itsyourmoney.ie.

Our home was badly damaged in the recent floods (2011). What financial help can we get pending the processing of our insurance claim?
In 2009, the Government allocated a sum of €10 million to fund a Humanitarian Assistance Scheme for people affected by the recent flooding. The scheme, which is means tested, provides emergency financial assistance to households who are not in a position to meet costs for essential needs in the period immediately following flooding. The aim of the scheme is to provide financial support to people whose homes are damaged by flooding. The scheme includes assistance for basic essential items such as carpets, flooring, furniture, household appliances and bedding (and possibly some structural damage). In addition, financial assistance may be available pending the approval of your insurance claim. This payment may

be requested to be refunded on receipt of your insurance claim. For further details, contact your local Department of Social Protection representative (formerly known as community welfare officers) in your local Health Centre.

As an employee, what are my rights if I can't get to work because of snow or frost?

There is no legislation specifically in this area therefore as an employee you are obliged to turn up for work. Your employer may grant discretion such as a day's leave, time in lieu owed or other local arrangements. Alternatively, an employer may impose disciplinary action for absenteeism from work. If you have an accident travelling to work there is a scheme called Injury Benefit. This benefit and payment from the Department of Social Protection protects employees going to and from and in work. It is available to the majority of employees and only covers an illness if it will last for more than three days (up to a maximum of 26 weeks). Any medical costs related to the injury are covered under the Medical Care Scheme.

What responsibility do I have regarding risk of accident outside my home or business, for instance people falling on ice?

Some house insurance policies have addition clauses to cover liability for visitors' accidents on your property. However, the principle of the duty of care is also a consideration. The general duty is to act as a reasonable person, in accordance with standards of care or conduct. Another consideration is whether the damage or injury is or could be reasonably foreseeable if you do nothing or if you do not take reasonable care when clearing. Therefore, when clearing public areas or entrances, ensure you follow best practice and take all reasonable care not to cause further or alternative risk of injuries. This means taking proper care, e.g. do not use boiling water to clear a footpath if there is a prospect of further freezing, use proper salt or material to improve grip, or, if there is potential for injury, make sure you flag or indicate this in advance for all possible users. If you are in doubt about clearing public or private areas do not do anything to further increase the risk.

What if I have an accident in a shop or its car park?
There is a duty of care owed to visitors and all reasonable care must be taken to ensure the visitor does not suffer an injury. Disclaimer notices cannot remove risk completely and cannot allow the occupier to intentionally or recklessly cause injury or damage to a visit. Therefore all shop owners or retailers should take all reasonable and best practice care and maintenance to ensure customers or persons accessing or leaving your store or premises to prevent reasonable risk of damage to themselves or others.

I have a management company and it is not gritting the common areas. Does it have to do this?
Under the Property Services Regulation Act 2011 all property service providers must be registered and licensed to operate. In addition they must have professional indemnity in case of injury or risk to the public. The Property Services Regulation Authority must be satisfied the service provider has the competent skills to carry out the role.

Therefore (as discussed earlier in the section on management companies, see pp. 130–136) complaints can be made to the Regulator in relation to service providers and action can be taken by the Regulator to impose fines, imprisonment and removal of licences upon renewal if the complaint is well founded after investigation. The service provider, therefore, must comply with regulations and remove or reduce the risk of injury to the public, as they have a duty of care (as stated above). Complaints can be made to the Property Services Regulatory Authority at 1890-252712 or check the website at www.npsra.ie.

Equity Release

I have heard the ads on the radio about equity release, and releasing money tied up in my property. How much can I get? How much will it cost? And what are the implications for social welfare payments and my children's inheritance?

Equity release schemes are available to people over 55 who have money tied up in the value of their homes, and who wish to release it now instead of moving house and 'cashing in'. As the majority of people at this stage of their life are mortgage free, a percentage value of their home can be cashed in now. There are two main types of equity release:

- Lifetime mortgage scheme.
- Home reversion schemes.

Lifetime Mortgage Scheme

This scheme allows you to borrow money against the market value of your home. You make no repayments now and continue to live in your home, and the loan is repaid against the market value of your home when you die or move out (this may include moving to a nursing home or into long-term care if greater than six months). The

maximum loan is generally less than half the market value
of the home now. It can be paid in a lump sum or instalments; fees may vary. If the property is jointly owned, the
mortgage must be paid when the remaining borrower dies
or moves out permanently.

The interest is usually higher than on normal mortgages
(fixed or variable rates). Interest is charged on the amount
you borrow and increases over time (compound interest). There is a major risk that the longer the time period,
the higher the amount due. The case may emerge that
the mortgage due is greater than the market value of the
house when you die unless you ensure there is a 'no nega-
tive equity guarantee' clause in your agreement. This will
ensure you will not be liable for any costs other than the
value of your home. You may be forced to sell your home
if you are absent for more than six months, do not insure
your home or do not maintain it to a normal standard.

Home Reversion Schemes

These schemes allow you to sell a share (percentage) of
your house in return for a set cash price now in a lump
sum. The cash lump sum amount may be less than half
the current actual market value rate. Percentage shares
available vary depending on your age and the market
value of your home. You can remain living in your home
for the rest of your life. The older you are, the greater the
actual cash value of the percentage share you receive. This
is mainly due to the fact that your life span decreases as
you get older (it varies for men and women). There are
two types of percentage share – fixed and variable. A fixed
share is where you agree to sell a specific percentage share
regardless of how long you live. Alternatively, you could

consider a 'variable share' contract, where the percentage share owned by the company automatically increases every year you live, but the amount of the lump sum you receive now is bigger than the fixed share.

You must also consider any implications for social welfare payments. If you are in receipt of a means-tested payment (non-contributory), the Department of Social Protection must be informed of any cash or savings you receive. Payments or savings over €20,000 (€50,000 if you are on Disability Allowance payment) are allowable. Payments or savings in excess of these rates will affect your weekly social welfare payment. If you do not advise social welfare of your windfall, they may be able to seek a refund of payments due after your death, and before the distribution of any inheritance.

You must also consider the implications in relation to any proposed inheritance you may wish to be distributed, as the value of such inheritance may vary depending on the scheme selected. In some cases there may not be any inheritance left from your property. Therefore, in summary, it is advisable to fully research all schemes and their terms and conditions, ensure the financial provider is registered and regulated by the Central Bank, and also seek independent legal advice. All details regarding the product should be fully and clearly explained to you in full, such as costs, implications, etc. If you are unhappy or have a complaint in relation to any equity release product it is firstly advisable to make a complaint to the relevant financial provider directly. Each financial provider is required to comply with the Central Bank's Consumer Protection Code. If you are still unhappy with the response you can make a complaint to the Financial Ombudsman (see Chapter 2, p. 89).

If you are considering equity release to pay for nursing home fees, you may wish to consider the Nursing Home Support Scheme. State financial support is available if a person cannot meet the full cost of care (means tested). You must be ordinarily resident in Ireland, i.e. living here for at least twelve months, and have been assessed for need of care (under the care needs assessment). Approved nursing homes include public, private and voluntary nursing homes taking part in the scheme. Since 1 July 2009 the National Quality Standards for Residential Care Settings for Older People in Ireland has been in effect and is enforced by the Health Information and Quality Authority (HIQA).

Since 2009, a new financial assessment for both public and private nursing homes has been introduced (Guide to a Fair Deal, commonly known as the 'Fair Deal Scheme') under the Nursing Home Support Scheme Act 2009. The means test will simply be 80 per cent of the applicant's disposable income. Applicants can include couples, including same-sex couples (residing together for three years) and civil partners. The applicant, if single and only on a social welfare payment, must retain a minimum of €43.80 per week. If married or cohabiting, the other party must have at least €219 per week (the maximum rate of the State (Non-Contributory) Pension or 50 per cent of the couple's income available). Cash assets are assessed to include monies in accounts, in cash, monies lent (and repayable), stocks, shares, bonds and transferred cash assets. Other relevant assets include the family home, property, farms, shops, and businesses or other commercial premises (less borrowings or maintenance of property). The value of assets at the time of assessment is at market rates. Assets (or cash) transferred, disposed of or sold in the previous five years (prior to 9 October 2008) for less than 75 per cent of their market value (excluding that related to maintenance claims, separation, divorce or inheritance) may have to be considered. Transfers of a farm or business, prior to or due to an illness or disability which caused a person to need care, are limited to the previous three years. A substantial part of the relevant partner's/civil partner's working day must be or have been regularly and consistently managing the farm or business.

The first €36,000 (single person) or €72,000 (couple) of assets are excluded. The balance of the value of the assets is assessed at 5 per cent of their value. Each person in the couple is assumed to own half of all assets. In all other cases the assessable rate for a single person of their private residence is 5 per cent per year for a maximum of three years, i.e. 15 per cent (regardless of whether a person is in care for a longer period). For couples or co-owners the maximum rate is 7.5 per cent. The charge from the assessment can be paid at the time of assessment or may be deferred until the sale of assets, the death of the person in care or the death of other family members.

Alternatively, a person could apply for a nursing home loan from the HSE (if he or she is ineligible for State support). To be eligible, he or she must have an asset (excluding cash) against which the loan can be charged (similar to a mortgage). This loan payment is then paid upon a specified event, e.g. death, and the loan is deducted (as a primary loan) from the estate before the distribution of inheritance. The interest of the loan is chargeable at the rate of the consumer price index. If you sell the asset, the loan is repayable immediately. The HSE must be notified of the sale of a chargeable asset within ten days. A postponement of the loan payment can be requested (within three months or no later than six months after the death, subject to a valid reason). This postponement can only be applied for by a connected person (i.e. a person who has resided in the concerned premises for three years prior to the person entering the nursing home). The connected person must not have any financial interest in any other property and may be a child (under the age of 21), a sibling, a co-owner, someone in receipt of a carer's payment for the person needing care for the six-month period prior to him or her entering a nursing home, or a person in receipt of a long-term disability payment or State Pension no greater than the maximum State Pension (Contributory) rate. If approved, the new (postponed) loan must be paid for within twelve months of the connected person's death, or within six months of the sale of the asset (interest is chargeable on late payments). Revenue has the power to collect the outstanding payment due for a twelve-year period from the time the amount becomes due. This payment is known as a deferred charge.

Chapter 4

General Citizens' Rights

Begging

I am constantly being harassed by beggars at the ATM. Are there any rules to prevent this?

The Criminal Order (Public Justice) Act 2011 prohibits harassment, intimidation, soliciting money or obstruction of members of the public by persons who engage in begging in or around an ATM, 'nightsafe' or public buildings. In addition, it gives powers to An Garda Síochána to prevent begging and also to prevent 'organised' begging. The penalties for an individual beggar is a €500 fine, arrest and/or one month in prison. For 'organised' begging, that is, a person who controls, directs or forces persons to beg, the penalties are a fine of between €5,000 and €200,000 or arrest and between twelve months' and five years' imprisonment. The Gardaí now have the power to request the person begging to move away from the place, and will have the power to issue on-the-spot fines if the action does not cease.

Change of Name

I have just entered a civil partnership and want to change my surname. What do I need to do?

A change of name can occur through common usage, i.e. by informing relevant organisations or individuals of your details, i.e. doctor, dentist, pharmacist, etc. Upon marriage or civil partnership, there is no legal requirement to change your surname (this is mainly done for convenience purposes). The only way to legally change your name is by deed poll.

A deed poll is a signed declaration that binds a person from the date of signing. A deed poll for a change of name contains declarations (sworn statement or affidavit) that you are abandoning the use of your old name, that you will use your new name at all times and that you require everyone to use your new name.

This declaration (deed poll) does not change any original birth certificate but simply allows you to add a certificate to your original birth certificate. A change of name by deed poll can be done yourself or, if you wish, by a solicitor. The stamp duty fee is €32 for a deed poll (an additional fee may be required to receive a sworn declaration from your solicitor or Commissioner for Oaths). Further information can be obtained from the deed poll section, Four Courts, Dublin 7 (01-8886000).

Regarding changing a child's surname, while it is a simple matter to add a father's details to a birth certificate, a father's details cannot be removed thereafter. Therefore, if a child's surname is that of his or her mother, it can only be changed to the father's name if the father's details were not originally added to the birth certificate or if the surname can be re-registered with the consent of both parents. Also, a child's name can be changed by common usage or deed poll. The Civil Registration (Amendment) Bill proposes to reform legislation relating to general rights, non-marital fathers and grandparents, including the possibility of compulsory joint registration of births where parents are not married. It will also validate embassy marriages/civil partnerships, deal with marriages of convenience and make certain other changes to the Civil Registration Act 2004.

Children aged between fourteen and seventeen can execute a deed poll themselves but need the consent of both parents. If a child is under the age of fourteen, a parent can execute a deed poll but still needs the consent of the other parent.

Credit History

I was recently turned down for a loan but I can't understand why this happened. Would I be blacklisted? Can I find out?
Yes, you can request a search of your credit history from the Irish Credit Bureau (ICB) for €6. This can be done online or in writing. The report contains information on personal details, loans, repayments, missed payments, settlements and/or legal action. The ICB (www.icb.ie), can be contacted at 01-2600388. Among ICB members are financial institutions, some credit unions and local authorities. Utility companies are excluded, e.g. the ESB.

The search will provide you with information on your credit history for the last five years. This report will show any financial institutions that accessed your file in the last twelve months. If you feel the report is wrong, correction may be brought to the attention of the ICB. Such complaints may have to be investigated further (by the Financial Regulator). If the company you applied to did not access your file, you may consider taking a case to the Data Protection Commissioner.

If the file is correct and you had a dispute with a financial institution in the past, you may be able to add a 200-word reason for that situation. Alternatively, you can simply wait five years, as after such time details of a defaulted loan will be deleted from the record.

The EU Directive on consumer credit agreements (Directive 2008/48/EC) implemented in Ireland by European Communities (Consumer Credit Agreements) Regulations 2010 (SI 281/2010), provides that financial providers, before agreeing to give you a loan, are obliged to assess your creditworthiness based on information obtained from you. It also provides that, if you are refused credit because of the information found, the financial provider must immediately tell you this and give you details of the information found. This applies to personal consumer credit agreements for amounts between €200 and €75,000 (excluding mortgages). It is proposed to regulate credit rating and credit reference agencies at EU level (SEC (2008) 2745/6) as these are not currently regulated. The focus of the proposal is to introduce a legally binding registration and surveillance regime for credit rating agencies issuing credit ratings.

Data Protection

Can I have incorrect information in my files corrected or deleted?
Yes, if you find information in your file that is incorrect or irrelevant, you can ask the data controller (company

controlling information) to rectify it. This remit comes under the Data Protection Act 2003. Complaints in relation to inaccurate data may be made to the Data Protection Commissioner (www.dataprotection.ie).

Can I request a company to provide me with information held on file belonging to me?
Yes, you can do so by forwarding an application to the relevant body requesting a copy of information held on computer or manual files about you, under the Data Protection Acts 1998–2003. You may need to include personal information to identify yourself clearly. Such requests must be responded to within 40 days.

Debt Collection

I have a debt collector calling to my home continuously. Can I do anything about this?
Section 11 of the Non-Fatal Offences against the Person Act 2007 states:

A person who makes any demand for a payment of a debt shall be guilty of an offence if

- *The demands by reason of their frequency are calculated to subject the debtor or a member of the family of the debtor to alarm, distress or humiliation, or*
- *The person falsely represents that criminal proceedings lie for non-payment of debt, or*
- *The person falsely represents that he or she is authorised in some official capacity to enforce payment, or*
- *The person utters a document falsely represented to have an official character.*

Such an offence can be punishable in the District Court by a fine or conviction. If you find this is the case, you should report the matter to the local Gardaí.

Driving in Ireland

What is the situation now with learner permit licences? Who must travel with a learner? When can I apply for the driving test and how much is it?
Since 30 June 2008 all provisional driving licence holders must be accompanied at all times by a driver who has been a full driving licence holder for at least two years. The new laws are set down in the Road Traffic (Licensing of Drivers) Regulation 1999 (SI 352/99).

Under the changes, holders of the new provisional licences (now called learner permits) issued since the 30 October 2007 must always be accompanied by a full driving licence holder of at least two years. Since 11 June 2001 new drivers must have a theory test certificate before seeking a first learner permit (valid for two years). The theory test has been updated and revised since October 2011. Since 1 January 2003, all drivers are required to carry their driving licence with them at all times. A third permit will not be issued unless you have undergone a test in the last two years (if so, you will be issued with a two-year permit), or a test is forthcoming (if so, you will be issued with a one-year permit). Current provisional driving licences will continue to be valid until they expire. If your provisional licence expired five years ago you must undergo a Driver Theory Test before a new permit is issued. A new learner permit costs €15. If you have moved address, there is no charge for updating your licence.

The youngest age a person can apply for the theory test is fifteen (for Category B – car) but the earliest you can apply for the learner permit is age seventeen (Category B). You must submit a copy of your theory test certificate within two years of completion as if you do not you will need to repeat the test. There is no maximum age for applying. The driver theory test costs €45 (since April 2012). To appeal the decision, payment of an additional €45 is required; if successful on appeal this payment will be refunded to you. If you lose your theory test certificate, a duplicate can be requested for a fee of €15. For further information see www.theorytest.ie.

Since December 2007, you cannot take a driving test for at least six months after getting your first learner permit. Since February 2011, the fee for a driving test has increased to €85 for a car (Category B) and €120 for a truck or bus (Categories C and D). The test now requires both technical questions about the vehicle, i.e. parts etc., and a practical assessment. Ten days' notice must be given if you wish to postpone your test. A maximum of two post-ponements is possible after which your test fee is forfeited. A full ten-year driving licence costs €25. The Road Traffic Bill proposes to centralise the driver licensing function to the Road Safety Authority.

Since 1 February 2002, motorists over the age of 70 can get their full driving licence renewed for free, subject to the completion of a certification of fitness by your doctor.

Since 28 January 2010, a new provision exists to facili-tate the mutual recognition of driving disqualifications between Ireland and the UK. It is proposed that a new EU driving licence will come into effect by 2012 and exist-ing driving licences issued by each member state will be phased out by 2032.

I have a full driving licence from Poland. Will I have to sit a new driving test?

No, if you have a valid driving licence from an EU state (as well as other recognised countries) you will not have to re-sit the test, and you can exchange your licence for an Irish licence. The fee is €25 (for a ten-year licence), and you will be required to complete a D900 form (available from www.dublincity.ie).

What are penalty points and how are they stored?

Penalty points were introduced in 2002 (under the Road Traffic Act 2002). Penalty points do not physically appear on your licence but are recorded centrally. No driver in Ireland is allowed drive a vehicle while holding twelve current penalty points. Any driver that receives twelve penalty points in any three-year period will be automatically faced with a six-month disqualification. Penalty points apply to both full, provisional and learner permit licences. Penalty points may be added to your Irish licence if you held a foreign licence. They may be recognised across all EU states as part of the Convention of Driving Disqualification adopted by the EU in 1998 (although not in operation yet). Penalty points remain on your licence for a three-year period. If an offence took place in your car, but you were not driving at the time, you can submit the original penalty points notice with the details of the person driving to the original Garda station for re-issue to the person who was driving the car at the time the offence took place.

Generally, each offence carried a fixed charge and penalty points. Some serious offences carry a mandatory court appearance. The fixed fine fee generally increases if it is not paid within a certain period of time. If you do not pay the fine and the matter is referred to court, the fine and number of penalty points may be increased upon hearing. Driving convictions by the District Court are automatically forwarded to the RSA (Road Safety Authority) to be recorded on the 'Pulse' system (Garda system). Penalty point records are held on the National Vehicle and Driver File operated by the Department of Transport, Sports and Tourism. If you received notification that you have been disqualified for driving, you are obliged to surrender your licence at your local Motor Tax Office.

Penalty points can apply to a vast array of offences, including:

- Speeding.
- Seatbelt offences.
- Careless or dangerous driving.
- Vehicles offences – in relation to motor insurance, national car testing (NCT), etc.
- Driving whilst holding a mobile phone.
- Non-compliance with the 'Rules of the Road'.
- Drink driving.

A full list of penalty point offences can be found on www. penaltypoints.ie. You can at any stage find out how many penalty points you have by contacting the RSA at 1890-416141 and providing them with your licence number.

How long has the NCT been in operation? How often do I have to get my car tested?
Compulsory car testing has been in operation in Ireland since 2000 (as part of a European-wide directive). The NCT is carried out across a large number of centres nationwide on behalf of the Government. Since 2002 onwards, all cars

four years old and over are tested. Vehicles that pass the test will have to undergo a test every two years thereafter. Since June 2011, cars over ten years old are tested each year. Additional items for testing have been added since 1 January 2012 as per EU Directive 2010/48/EU.

The NCT costs €55. You must bring your vehicle registration/licensing certificate with you to the test centre. You are also required to produce your driving licence or passport as identification. If your car fails the test, you must book a re-test within 21 days and the re-test must be completed within 30 days of the original test date. A re-test costs €28. Re-tests that do not require the use of test equipment are free, including re-tests for minor visual items such as the replacement of a windscreen wiper. According to the National Car Testing Service Customer Charter, if you request an NCT appointment and it cannot be provided within four weeks, you are entitled to have the test carried out for free.

Vehicles imported to Ireland from outside the State (including Northern Ireland) must also go through the NCT once the vehicle is four years old or more. This applies, even if the vehicle previously received an MOT (UK) or any other vehicle test abroad. If the imported vehicle is already four years old or more when imported, it must go through the NCT immediately.

If you cancel your confirmed appointment with less than five working days' notice or if you do not turn up for your test, you will be charged an extra €22 (on top of the usual fee) when you next bring your vehicle for testing. Replacement NCT certificates are available for a fee of €12.70. You can appeal the decision of the NCT through their appeal system. You will be required to pay an additional full fee but if your appeal is successful you will receive a refund.

Appointments can be made online at www.ncts.ie or phone contacting 1890-200670.

First Aid

I have just completed my first aid training but am concerned that if I try to help and do something wrong I could be sued. Am I protected?
The Civil Law (Miscellaneous Provision) Act 2010 (Part 3, section 4) protects from liability those who give assistance to others who may be ill or injured as a result of an accident or other emergency. This legislation ensures that those who intervene to give help to others, and who offer this assistance in good faith, cannot then be penalised or held liable as a result of their intervention, unless in a case of gross negligence. Assistance, advice and care are defined as administering first aid and/or using an automated external defibrillator (AED), or the transport of a person from the scene of emergency to a hospital or other place to receive care. Section 51(d) states:

(1) A good Samaritan shall not be personally liable in negligence for any act done in an emergency when providing (a) assistance, advice or care to a person who is (i) in serious and imminent danger, or apparently in serious and imminent danger, of being injured or further injured, (ii) injured or apparently injured, or (iii) suffering, or apparently suffering, from an illness, or (b) advice by telephone or by another means of communication to a person (whether or not the person is a person referred to in paragraph (a)) who is at the scene of the emergency.

Freedom of Information

I want to receive a copy of medical information held about me on file in the hospital. How can I do this?
Public hospitals, government departments and other publicly funded bodies are covered under the Freedom of Information (FOI) Act 2003. Private hospitals or the Gardaí are not covered under the FOI Act. The FOI Act gives rights to the general public to gain access in a choice of formats to personal material (since 21 April 1998) recorded on file about themselves and the activities of the above organisations (section 15 and 16 reports) as covered by the Ombudsman. Such records can include information on computers, in manual files, on printouts, etc.

To seek a copy of your file, you must make an application in writing to the relevant body requesting a copy of your records under section 7 of the FOI Act. It is important to detail clearly the specific information you are looking for (from specific periods or specific events/operations) and in what format you require it, i.e. paper or digital. There is no fee for the provision of information, although a small administration fee may apply if excessive or additional work is required to locate such information, or if excessive paper is required.

What bodies are covered under the Freedom of Information Act?
All Government and Government-funded bodies are covered, including the HSE, city, town and county councils, public hospitals, mental health services, services for persons with intellectual disabilities, courts and educational institutions. The Ombudsman (Amendment) Bill 2008 proposes to widen the remit of the Ombudsman to

include a range of additional bodies and make changes to the administrative process.

Is my GP covered under the Freedom of Information Act?
No, private GPs are not covered under the FOI Act (although you could request your files under Data Protection), but Medical Card patients who attend a GP are entitled to access their files.

What happens after I send the letter? How quickly should I get a reply?
Your letter of application should be acknowledged within two weeks of being received and should be responded to within four weeks. An additional three weeks may apply if a third party is involved.

I sent my application five weeks ago and received no acknowledgement. What should I do?
If you have not received a reply within four weeks of your application, it is presumed your request was refused. You can then apply for re-examination by a senior member of the relevant organisation following the above guidelines. A response should be provided within three weeks.

If you are unhappy with the response, i.e. refusal of information, costs or information, you may request a re-examination. You can forward your original FOI request, with specific focus on the grounds of your disappointment or concerns. A response should be provided within three weeks.

What if I am still unhappy? To whom can I complain and who will help me?
If you are still unhappy with any aspect of your application or response, you can make a complaint to the Information Commissioner. The Information Commissioner will investigate the grounds of your complaint, follow up your dispute with the relevant body and try to resolve the access or other issue in relation to your request. Complaints should be made within six months of your initial application to the public body for your FOI request. For further information, call 1890-223030 or contact the Office of the Information Commissioner at info@oic.ie (www.oic.gov.ie).

I want to find out information on my file regarding who reported me to Social Welfare. Can I do this?
No, it is not possible to gain non-personal information that contains reference to other named parties sensitive to your file.

Ombudsman

What if I want to question a decision regarding my case made by a local authority? To whom can I complain?
First, you should appeal the decision to your local authority. Normally local authorities have a customer charter in place regarding time frames for investigation of complaints and responses. Second, if you are unhappy with the decision, the Ombudsman may investigate complaints by members of the public in relation to public bodies, i.e. government departments, local authorities, the HSE and An Post. The Ombudsman can examine decisions, refusals and administrative procedures of public bodies. (Exceptions may apply in relation to certain decisions, i.e.

private services, clinical judgments, court actions, Garda decisions or actions.) Complaints in relation to the Gardaí can be made to the Garda Ombudsman (www.gardaombudsman.ie) and complaints must be made within six months of the incident.

The role in assessing a decision or refusal is to ensure such action was fair and reasonable and without negligence. Complaints must be made within twelve months of the original complaint. Upon investigation, the Ombudsman will make a decision. This decision cannot be forced on a body, but it can be reported to the Houses of the Oireachtas.

There is no cost for this service. Complaints can be made to the Office of the Ombudsman (1890-223030; ombudsman@ombudsman.gov.ie; www.ombudsman.irlgov.ie).

Irish Citizenship

Our child was born on 10 January 2005 in Ireland. We are both non-Irish nationals and have been living here for three years. What is status of our child in terms of citizenship? Can I apply for Irish citizenship?

In June 2004, a referendum (Citizenship Act 2004) was passed by the people of Ireland to change the existing criteria for citizenship. The rule now states that children born after 1 January 2005 in Ireland to non-Irish national parents are not automatically entitled to Irish citizenship. One of the parents of a child must be an Irish national at the time the child is born. Under the Civil Law (Miscellaneous) Act 2011, civil partners have the same rights and entitlements as married couples. The Civil Registration Amendment Bill will also validate embassy marriages/civil partnerships.

Non-Irish national parents of children born in Ireland on or after 1 January 2005 must prove they have a genuine link to Ireland, i.e. they were legally in Ireland for three out of the previous four years immediately before the birth of the child. If this can be proven, their child will be entitled to Irish citizenship. Time spent in Ireland as students or asylum seekers will not be included in the calculation. To become an Irish citizen through naturalisation, i.e. being resident here, you have to:

- Reside in Ireland for a period of five of the previous nine years and have one year's continuous reckonable residence before the date of your application.
- Be eighteen years or older.
- Be of good character.
- Prove you can support yourself and your family financially (it may assist your case if you have not availed of State support in the previous three years).
- Intend in good faith to continue to reside in the State.
- Make a declaration of fidelity to the nation and loyalty to the State.

Your application can only be made on the completion of your fifth year in Ireland (you must show reckonable residence, i.e. documented residency). Since November 2011 there is a €175 fee for all new applications. A revised application (since November 2011) is available from the Citizenship Section (Naturalisation) of the Department of Justice, Equality and Law Reform or from www.inis. gov.ie. Applications can take in the region of 23 months to be processed from the date of receipt (since November 2011). You can decide to have dual citizenship but this is not always recognised by all countries so it is important to explore all your legal options first as this may impact on your rights in relation to travel and residency.

Money Advice

Since I lost my job, I don't know where to turn. We are in arrears with our mortgage and we are concerned about repossession. Is there any organisation that can help?
The Money Advice and Budgeting Service (MABS) is a national body that provides free, confidential and independent services to people who are in debt, or in danger of getting into debt. MABS can be contacted at 1890-283438 (9.00 a.m.–8.00 p.m., Monday–Friday), or you can contact your local office (contact details on www.mabs.ie).

It is important to review all your incomes and outgoings, and develop a 'budget' plan (a handy weekly spending diary, personal budget sheet and information booklet are available online or by post). You will also need to prioritise your debt, i.e. mortgage, electricity, etc., so it is therefore advisable to contact all your creditors and explain your situation as soon as possible. In many cases, creditors (people to whom you owe money) will be willing to develop a planned payment approach. It is important that this plan is realistic and you comply with the payment plan. If you foresee difficulty in making the agreed payments, it is advisable to contact the creditor prior to further difficulties arising.

In conjunction with MABS, it would be advisable to contact your local Citizens Information Centre to see if there are any areas of financial support available to you. You can contact your local MABS service and they can arrange an appointment for you to see one of their professional money advisors. In conjunction with the money advisor they will develop a budget and payment plan and liaise with your creditors. Therefore it is advisable to contact them as soon as possible and especially if major difficulties arise. The MABS service works closely with Department of Social Protection representatives (formerly known as community welfare officers (CWOs)) and St Vincent de Paul.

The Financial Regulator code of conduct on mortgage arrears (CCMA) was recently revised (January 2011). The new requirements are that a Mortgage Arrears Resolution Process (MARP) be used when dealing with arrears and pre-arrears customers. The five steps of MARP are: (1) communication (clear and consumer friendly); (2) financial information in booklet form and on the company's website providing clear contact points and support website links; (3) assessment; (4) resolution; and (5) appeals. In Budget 2012 the Minister announced that payment of the Mortgage Interest Supplement will be deferred for twelve months while the person engages in the MARP. In addition, an Arrears Support Unit (ASU) will be established by financial providers to assess arrears and pre-arrears cases. Customers may appeal MARP or ASU decisions to the internal Appeals Board. This appeals process replaces the complaints process under the Consumer Protection Code.

In return, lenders have agreed not to contact the customer unsolicited more than three times, by whatever means, in a calendar month other than correspondence required in compliance with regulations. The agreement also states that the lender cannot force a borrower to change from an existing tracker mortgage to another mortgage type as part of any alternative arrangement offered in arrears or pre-arrears.

Previously, the original CCMA (February 2009) allowed lenders to take legal action only after a six-month period, and the protection related to the primary residence only. AIB and Bank of Ireland (recapitalised banks) did not take court action until after twelve months of arrears (presuming you had continued to co-operate with the bank). In addition, the protocol between twelve credit institutions and MABS had been agreed. The protocol set down new joint procedures to help manage debt. In February 2010, the Statutory Code of Conduct on Mortgage Arrears changed to require that a regulated lender must wait at least twelve months from the time arrears first arise before applying to the courts for legal action on repossession. Some lenders not covered by this code may choose to abide but are not obliged to do so.

Repossession orders should be the last decision only if all other avenues have been explored in full, and ongoing communication between the lender and consumer have fully broken down. The Financial Regulator's statutory Consumer Protection Code, implemented by lenders since 1 June 2008, ensures that lenders act fairly, honestly, professionally and in the best interests of their customers. The Code also requires that customers are informed in writing of the status of their loans and/or arrears as soon as possible. In addition, since 1 January 2012 the Code has been revised to regulate banks, insurance and investment companies and intermediaries. This includes assistance with arrears handling, banning 'doorstep' visits and unsolicited selling of financial products, restrictions on the number of contacts (as per the CCMA ruling above) and better 'matching' of products to a customer's needs. In addition, there are greater controls in place in relation to mortgage applications and a requirement for full transparency of benefits, risk and all hidden costs. The amended code also sets down specific time frames in relation to complaint handling. For further information, contact the Financial Regulator at 1890-777777 or check the website www.financialregulator.ie.

The Minister for Environment, Community and Local Government announced (in October 2011) the development of a pilot 'Mortgage to Rent' Scheme. Under this scheme, households in extreme mortgage distress, who are eligible for social housing, will be able to remain in their homes as social housing tenants with either the lending institution or a housing association taking ownership of the property.

TV Licence

Who needs a TV licence and what are the rules? If I watch the News on my laptop will I still have to pay?
Every household, business or institution in Ireland with a television or equipment capable of receiving a television signal (using an aerial, satellite dish, cable or other means), whether it is in use or not, is required by law to have a television licence. You do not require a television licence to watch television on your computer or mobile phone at present. However, you do require a licence if the computer is used together with any other apparatus to receive a signal. The television licence fee is collected by An Post on behalf of the Minister for Communications, Energy and Natural Resources. Part of the licence fee is granted to RTÉ to provide public service programmes, which includes the provision of radio and television services, with the purpose to entertain, educate, inform and cater for all members of the community, as well as providing news and current affairs programmes, including coverage of proceedings in the Houses of the Oireachtas and the

European Parliament. If you are in rented accommodation, the person residing in the property in possession of a television is responsible for the TV licence. One licence is sufficient if you have multiple TV sets in a private home. An individual licence is required if the building is in separate units, i.e. flats, bedsits or apartments. The cost of a licence fee is €160 per year. The fine for non-payment of a TV licence is €1,000 (first offence). This can increase to €2,000 for multiple offences.

It is proposed the TV licence will be replaced by a new Household Broadcasting Charge in 2014, regardless of equipment or an ability to receive signal, and will be chargeable to all households and businesses (similiar to current charging across certain EU states).

Analogue TV (provided by an aerial) will be switched off on 24 October 2012. To continue viewing, you will either need a saorview box or saorview TV. For further information, please check www.saorview.ie or phone 1890-222012.

Pets

I have a dog. How much is a dog licence? Can I take my pet on holiday with me abroad?
A dog licence is €20 per year (since January 2012) and is available from any post office. In many cases, renewal applications are now being administered by your local authority and can be renewed online. At all times your dog must have an identification tag (name and address) on its collar; failure to have this will result in a fine of €30. The same fine is applicable if the owner (aged sixteen or older) cannot produce the dog licence. Under section 22 of the Litter Pollution Act 1997, it is an offence for your dog

to foul in a public place. A fine of €150 is applicable. You can make a complaint to your local District Court in relation to breach of this law.

A EU pet passport is now available for cats, dogs and ferrets within EU member states. Since 1 January 2012 there will be harmonised conditions for pet dogs, cats and ferrets that travel throughout the entire EU. Pets entering Ireland from within the EU (including the UK) will now require a passport/certificate showing identification, proof of specific rabies vaccination at least 21 days before entry and proof of specific tapeworm treatment of all pet dogs. Previously the passport certified that the pet had been micro-chipped, blood-tested and vaccinated against rabies, and had been treated for ticks and tapeworm.

The pet must travel with you, must be older than three months old, and can only travel on an approved carrier and an approved route. For further information, contact the Department of Agriculture, Fisheries and Food (1890-200510) or check the website www.agriculture.gov.ie/pets.

Voting Rights

Who can vote in the next local and European elections in 2014 or if there is a referendum? How do I know if I am registered to vote? How can I add my name to the list?
People aged eighteen or over before polling day (proof required and completed form) can vote if they have been ordinarily resident in the State. Non-EU citizens may only vote in the local elections, whereas Irish, British and EU citizens can vote in both the European and local elections. Only Irish citizens can vote in a referendum. The register of electors (the book in which all voters are registered) should be available for inspection at your local authority office,

post office, Garda station or public library. Alternatively, you can check if you are registered on the website www. checktheregister.ie.

Any changes made to the register before 25 November each year will be noted in the amended register, which will be published on 1 February the following year and comes into effect on the 15 February. If you are not registered, or your circumstances have changed, you must complete an application form (RFA2) and return it to your local authority office. If you are on the register and have moved address, you must complete a RFA3 form or else you will have to vote at the polling station linked to your old address. Both forms must be stamped by your local Garda station or, if you have a disability, must be certified. All forms must be completed and returned to your local or city council fifteen days before the intended voting date (Sundays and public holidays are excluded in the 'counting' days). Postal votes are available to Irish diplomats (and their spouses) abroad, Gardaí, full-time members of the Defence Forces, or to persons who have a physical illness or disability, are studying at an educational institute, are in jail due to a court order or have a certain occupation. Postal votes are not available in general to Irish citizens living abroad or on holiday abroad, other than those listed above.

You should receive a voting card between two and five days before polling day. Photo ID should be brought to the polling station with your card. If you do not receive a polling card, and you are sure you are on the register of electors (or supplementary list), you simply go on the day to your local polling station with photo ID (passport or driving licence) to cast your vote. If there any problems on the day these must be discussed with the presiding officer in the polling station.

What is the procedure in voting and what happens if I spoil my vote?
In the Dáil, European and local elections the procedure is to write the number 1 beside your first choice of candidate, the number 2 beside your second choice of candidate and so on. If you place an 'X' beside your chosen candidate this may be classed as a 'spoilt' vote or the deciding officer could make the decision as to whether it was a mark of intent. It is essential that you check your voting card has been stamped before you vote, as unstamped voting cards are not counted. The returning officer declares the results of the election in each constituency. For referendum changes (votes to change the constitution), you can mark an 'X' beside your chosen decision, i.e. to accept the change or reject the change.

If you spoil your vote, which you may decide is your democratic choice, it will be excluded as invalid for counting purposes.

My son has a disability. Will he be restricted from voting? What if the polling station is inaccessible for him with his disability?
Once your son's name is on the register of electors or supplementary register, he has the right to vote. There is no restriction, regardless of physical or mental disability, in voting once you are on the list. Assistance is available on the day if required.

If the polling station is not accessible for your son, he can write to the Returning Officer no less than one week before polling day to request another accessible polling station in his constituency. Public notice of accessible polling stations will be available in the constituency. If approved, he will be given a written authorisation to use a more accessible polling station.

When must election posters be taken down?

Posters must be taken down within seven days of the election. On-the-spot fines of €150 can be imposed by the local authority for each poster.

Ward of Court

I am worried about my mother's mental health, and if she is of sound mind in making future financial decisions. What can you recommend?

You may wish to consider making your mother a 'ward of court'. This is required when a person is unable to manage their affairs due to a mental incapacity (this may also be applicable to persons under eighteen years of age). The court will be required to determine whether the person is of unsound mind and incapable of managing their own affairs. You will be required to make a petition to the High Court, with proof from two doctors. For further information, contact the Office of the Ward of Court or check www.courts.ie. The new Mental Capacity Bill proposes to replace the 'ward of court' and 'enduring power of attorney' system and to reform the law on mental capacity, taking into account the Law Reform Commission's Report on Vulnerable Adults and the Law.

An Enduring Power of Attorney is a legal document in which you give another person the power to make decisions on your behalf if you ever lose the capacity in the future to make decisions yourself. The new Bill proposes to consider the appointment of a 'guardian' in the best interest of the person. In addition, the Bill proposes to examine the necessary interventions as they arise, the person's 'best interest' and their capacity to understand. Hearings will be held in private with all relevant parties in attendance.